SPORTS ENCYCLOPEDIAS

THE PROFESSIONAL GOLF ENCYCLOPEDIA

BY CORBU STATHES

Encyclopedias

An Imprint of Abdo Reference

abdobooks.com

TABLE OF CONTENTS

INTRODUCTION

Some people believe the golf term *caddie* comes from the French military aides of Mary, Queen of Scots, who were called cadets.

HISTORY OF GOLF

Golf has a long history. Nobody knows exactly how the sport was created. Some people believe golf is as old as the Roman Empire. Others say it originated in China or continental Europe. Most people credit Scotland as the sport's birthplace.

Early Scottish players would hit pebbles over sand dunes and fields with bent sticks or clubs. In the mid-1400s, golf was so popular that

EARLY GOLF GEAR

Early golf clubs were made of beechwood with ash or hazel shafts. Balls were made of compressed feathers in stitched horsehide. The development of factories and machines made producing clubs and balls easier and cheaper. This made golf more accessible to everyday people.

people were playing it rather than doing their military training. Scotland's King James II banned the sport. However, most people ignored the ban.

In the early 1500s, King James IV began playing golf. Soon, royals spread the game to other places while traveling. King Charles I brought it to England. Mary, Queen of Scots, introduced it to France.

EARLY RULES AND COURSES

In 1744, the Honourable Company of Edinburgh Golfers wrote the first formal golf rules, the Thirteen Articles. These were used for a tournament at Leith Links in Edinburgh, Scotland.

At that time, each golf course had its own rules. The number of holes varied from course to course. The first 18-hole course was built in the Scottish town of St. Andrews in 1764. Eighteen holes soon became the standard for golf courses.

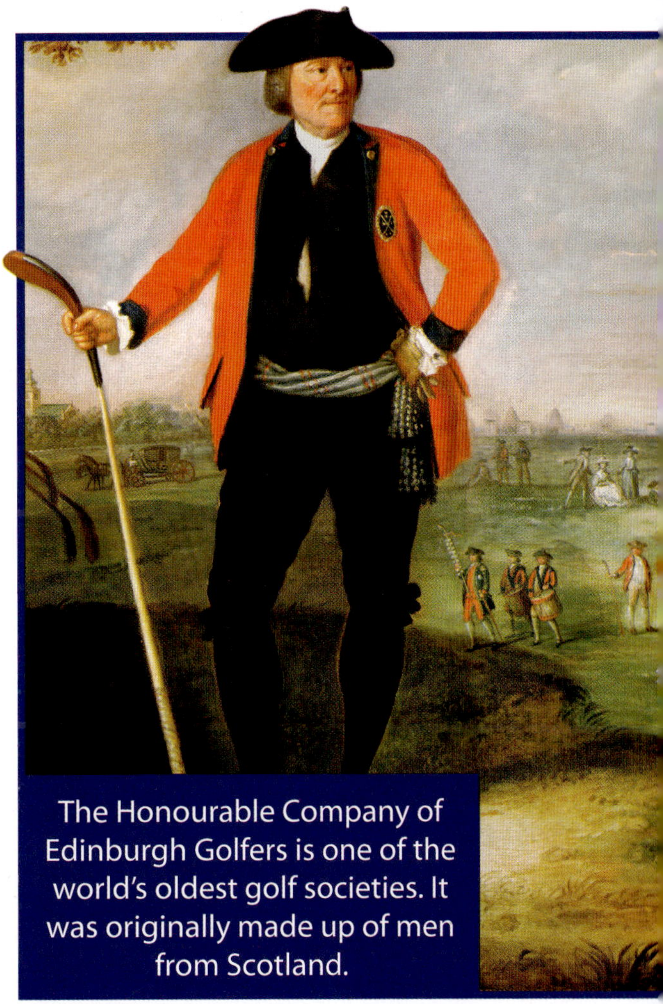

The Honourable Company of Edinburgh Golfers is one of the world's oldest golf societies. It was originally made up of men from Scotland.

GOLF IN AMERICA

Golf was introduced to North America long before the United States was established. The earliest golf reference in America comes from the 1600s. An ordinance in Fort Orange, New York, banned playing golf in the streets. In 1841, the first US golf group formed in South Carolina. It was called Harleston Green.

While people had been playing golf for several hundred years, there was no official organization for the game. Saint Andrew's Golf Club, founded in New York in 1888, is credited with starting organized golf in the United States. In 1893, the Chicago Golf Club was built. It was the country's first 18-hole course.

Saint Andrew's Golf Club in New York is one of the oldest golf clubs in the United States. Many influential Americans, such as businessman Andrew Carnegie, *right*, golfed at the club.

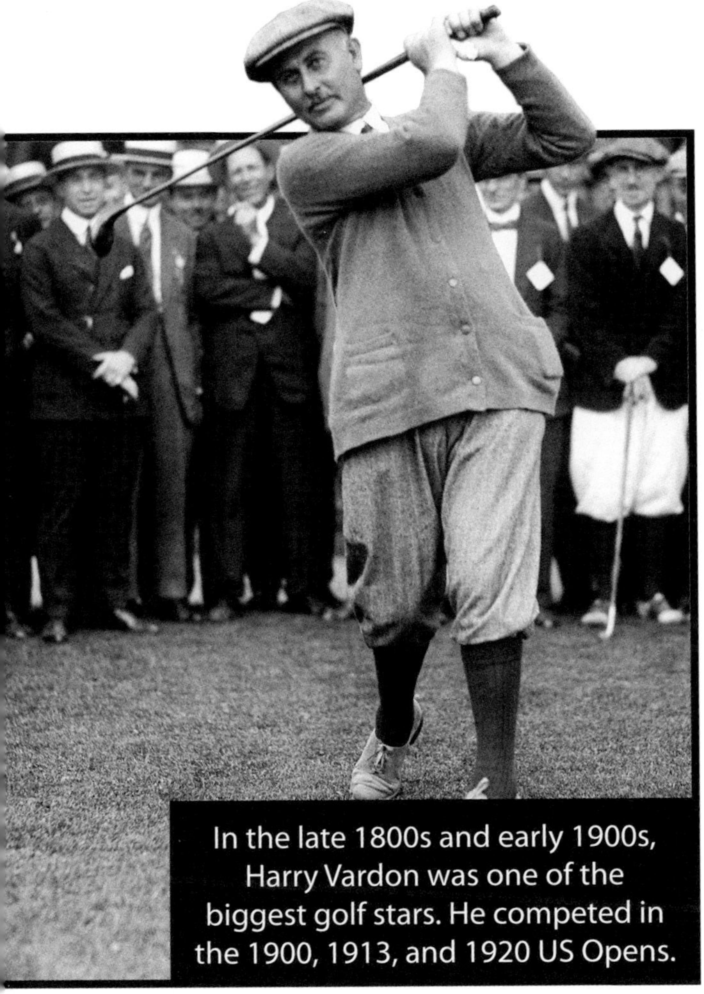

In the late 1800s and early 1900s, Harry Vardon was one of the biggest golf stars. He competed in the 1900, 1913, and 1920 US Opens.

The next year, the United States Golf Association (USGA) formed. It started three national championships: the Men's Amateur, Women's Amateur, and US Open. The first US Open took place in 1895. Soon, tournaments were held across the country. The first Western Open was held in Illinois in 1899. In Open events, golfers do not have to be professionals. Amateurs can also participate.

By 1900, there were more than 1,000 golf clubs in the United States. US golfers quickly gained attention. In 1911, John McDermott became the first American-born player to win the US Open. This increased national interest in golf.

A nationwide exhibition tour by English golf stars Harry Vardon and Ted Ray drew more attention to the sport. When the two golfers lost the US Open in a playoff to amateur Francis Ouimet, golf was thrust into the spotlight. Strong commercial interest followed, meaning there was money to be won. The United States soon became the center of professional golf.

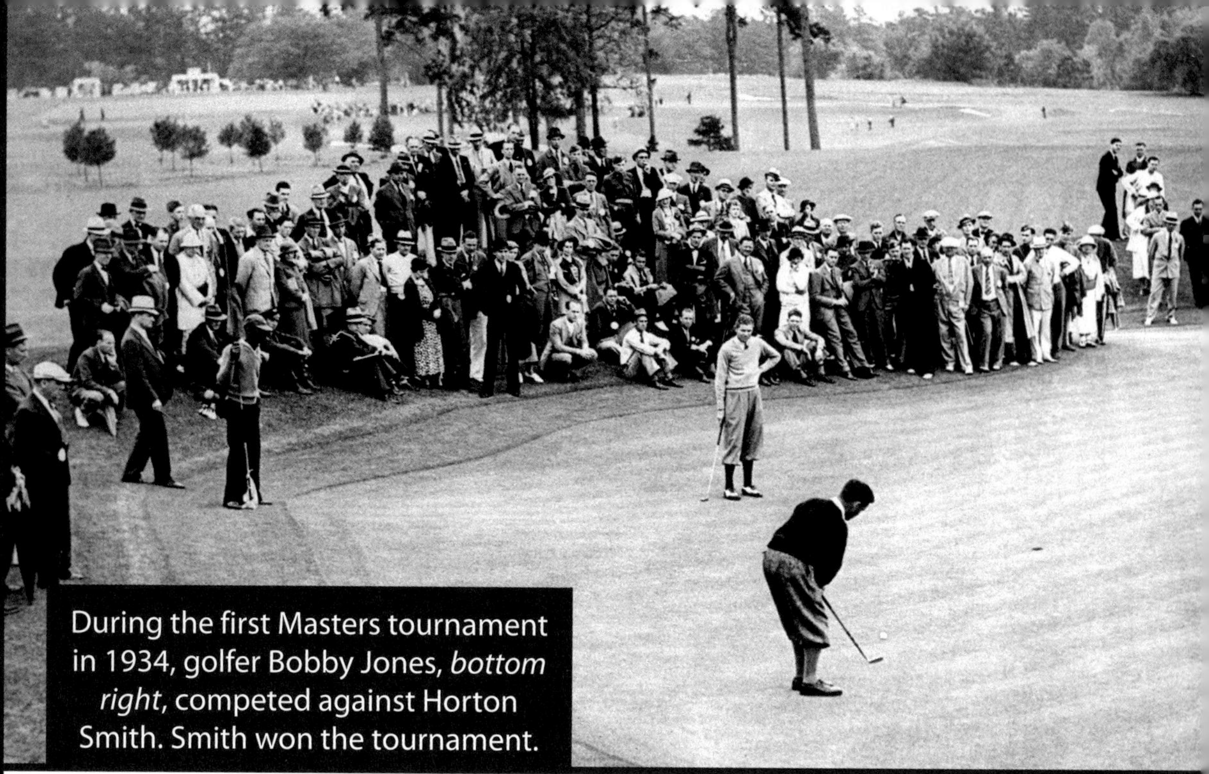

During the first Masters tournament in 1934, golfer Bobby Jones, *bottom right*, competed against Horton Smith. Smith won the tournament.

ORGANIZED TOURS

Early organized golf was limited to white men, most of whom were wealthy. They played in tours, or series of tournaments. In the 1920s, tournaments were held in warmer states during winter. Golfers traveled from the West Coast to the East Coast. By the mid-1920s, the tour offered $77,000 in prize money. That's equal to about $1.3 million in 2024. In 1927, American and European teams began competing in the Ryder Cup.

In 1932, the first playing professionals organization formed. This separated professional golfers from amateurs in the USGA. The tour structure also became more organized. In 1934, the Augusta National Invitation Tournament began. Its name changed to the Masters in 1939. It became known as one of four major men's golf tournaments, or majors. In the late 1950s, networks began televising golf. This increased the sport's exposure, turning tour players into household names.

In 1968, the Professional Golfers' Association (PGA) Tour began. Over the next 25 years, the money the PGA Tour generated grew from almost $4 million to $229 million. The total purse for 45 events was $5 million in 1968. By 1993, it was ten times that.

Many people thought courses should be more fan friendly. At most courses, fans stood on flat ground and used periscopes to see over people. Tour Commissioner Deane Beman invented stadium golf courses. These offered better vantage points and layouts. In 1980, Beman oversaw the building of the first stadium course, TPC Sawgrass.

OFFICIAL MONEY

The Tour tracks how much money each player wins throughout the year. This is called Official Money. Whoever wins the most money wins the money title. In 1968, Billy Casper led that category with more than $200,000. Twenty years later, Curtis Strange became the Tour's first million-dollar earner. In 2023, Scottie Scheffler made more than $21 million.

TPC Sawgrass was constructed on 415 acres (168 ha) of swampland. Deane Beman designed the course so that it would suit a variety of playing styles.

During the late 1990s, Black golfer Tiger Woods dominated the golf world. From 1997 to 2009, he won the most money on the Tour nine out of thirteen times. By the end of 2009, Woods was third on the all-time Tour wins list. He not only broke records but also helped golf reach younger and more diverse audiences. Woods became world famous, inspiring a new generation of players. Meanwhile, golf prize money ballooned.

To add excitement to the end of the golf season, the FedEx Cup was created as a playoff system in 2007. Tour players earn points throughout the year based on where they finish in each tournament. The top point earners qualify for the playoffs. The top point earners in the playoffs move on to a final event. The FedEx Cup winner earns a large payout.

The PGA Tour was long considered the top pro golf tour. But in 2021, LIV Golf announced it would begin play the following year.

At age 21, Tiger Woods won the 1997 Masters by 12 strokes. This historic victory was the first major win of his career.

GOLF AT THE OLYMPICS

Golf was first included in the Summer Olympic Games in 1900 and 1904. But it was dropped from the list of Olympic sports until the 2016 Olympics. Since 2016, the Summer Olympics has featured two golf events: a men's individual stroke play tournament and a women's individual stroke play tournament. Each tournament includes four rounds. Gold medalists in these events have included Xander Schauffele, Justin Rose, Inbee Park, and Nelly Korda. At the 2024 Olympic Games in Paris, France, American Scottie Scheffler took home the gold in the men's event. It was his first time winning an Olympic medal. In the 2024 women's event, Lydia Ko of New Zealand won gold. It was her third Olympic medal, but her first time winning gold. Ko won bronze at the 2020 Olympics and silver at the 2016 Olympics.

The name "LIV" refers to the Roman numerals for 54, the number of holes played at LIV events. Unlike the PGA Tour, LIV guaranteed pay. PGA players had to qualify for a tournament's weekend rounds to assure themselves of pay. But LIV would have no cuts. It also offered more pay.

There was controversy around the new tour. Funding for LIV comes from Saudi Arabia's government-owned Public Investment Fund. Critics say this investment in sports is meant to cover up Saudi Arabia's poor record on human rights. Many golfers who decided to take the large sums of guaranteed money were also some of the more controversial PGA Tour players. This made LIV Golf a target for criticism. After two years of rivalry, the two tours formed a partnership in 2023.

Golfers Alice Bauer, Babe Didrikson Zaharias, Patty Berg, and Marlene Bauer, *left to right*, are among the 13 founders of the LPGA.

WOMEN'S TOURS

In the past, women had occasionally played in men's golf tournaments and tried to start their own tours. But they had long been excluded from professional sports and had to fight for places in the sports world. It wasn't until the Ladies Professional Golf Association (LPGA) was founded that women had an official organized tour. Thirteen players founded it in 1950. The founders included two major women's golf stars, Patty Berg and Babe Didrikson Zaharias. The founders not only played in LPGA tournaments but also helped organize them.

In its first year, the LPGA held 14 tournaments with $50,000 in prize money. By the end of the decade, it offered 26 tournaments and $200,000 in prize money. Nationally televised tournaments and corporate sponsorships soon followed. By the 1990s, the LPGA Tour had its first season with a million-dollar winner, Australian Karrie Webb.

The LPGA Tour grew beyond weekly tournaments too. The Solheim Cup started in 1990 as the women's version of the Ryder Cup. The LPGA also started an end-of-season tournament in 2006. Winners from the majors earned a berth in the LPGA Championship. That eventually turned into the CME Group Tour Championship, which had a points system similar to the FedEx Cup. In 2023, the LPGA Tour offered more than $100 million for the first time in its history. By 2024, the amount for the Tour Championship winner was $4 million.

Europe also developed a women's golf tour. The Ladies European Tour (LET) was founded in 1978. It joined forces with the LPGA Tour in 2020.

The US team won the first Solheim Cup in 1990. The team included nine golfers, including captain Kathy Whitworth, *center*.

THE PGA AND LPGA SEASON

Men's and women's professional golf are structured into annual seasons. These involve a series of scheduled events and tournaments. The PGA Tour's FedEx Cup runs from January through August, lasting the entire season. From 2013 to 2024, it overlapped the end of one year and the beginning of the next. In 2024, the Cup returned to a regular calendar-year schedule. At the start of each season, Tour members reset their FedEx Cup points and start at zero.

The schedule includes several types of tournaments. The majors are the

For the 2022–23 PGA Tour season, players who won majors were awarded 600 FedEx Cup points. Wyndham Clark won 600 points for winning the 2023 US Open.

biggest tournaments. There are four majors in the PGA season: the Masters, PGA Championship, US Open, and British Open. These take place in April, May, June, and July, respectively. The season also includes full-field events, which follow the historical structure of tournaments and have cuts after two days. Signature events have a limited field. They offer greater prize pools and more FedEx points.

The LPGA's points system is known as the Race to the CME Globe. When Michelle Wie West won the US Women's Open in 2014, she earned 625 points.

Players earn points based on how they do in tournaments. Majors award more points to players than regular Tour events do. The top 70 point earners qualify for the playoffs. The winner is then determined over three events. After the first event, the field is cut to 50 players. It is cut to 30 players for the final event, the Tour Championship. The FedEx Cup playoffs happen in August and September.

The LPGA schedule includes tournaments in the United States and several other countries. Players earn points based on their performances throughout the season. There are five major LPGA tournaments: the Chevron Championship, Women's PGA Championship, US Women's Open, Evian Championship, and Women's Open. The season ends with the Tour Championship in November.

TOURNAMENT PLAY STRUCTURE

To play in a tournament, golfers must qualify for it. To do so, they often need a Tour card. Players earn these at the Qualifying School, or Q-School. The top finishers and players who tie with them earn Tour status. Players can also obtain Tour cards by finishing near the top on smaller golf circuits.

Players without Tour cards may earn spots by playing in qualifying events on the Monday of the tournament week. Golfers can also play in tournaments through a sponsor exemption. This is when a tournament sponsor wants to include a golfer whose appearance will lead to ticket sales.

PGA Tour cards are usually engraved with a player's name and the PGA logo. In 2023, Ben Kohles earned a Tour card for the 2024 season.

PGA and LPGA tournaments usually last four days, spanning Thursday through Sunday. The first two rounds determine who makes it to the weekend rounds. Players with the best scores advance. The number of golfers who make the cut depends on the tournament. The standard is the top 65 players, along with ties. Players who do not advance get no money from the tournament. In 2023, the PGA announced it would hold several events with smaller fields and no cuts.

The first two rounds of a tournament are played in groups of three. The final rounds are played in pairs. For the first round, the most established players get the best tee times. Then it trickles down based on players' achievements. After cuts are made, players in last place tee off first. The top two scorers from the previous day tee off last.

If golfers tie at the end of a tournament, they play a specific number of holes to break the tie. If the score is still tied, the players go to sudden death. Other times, tiebreaker rounds begin with sudden death.

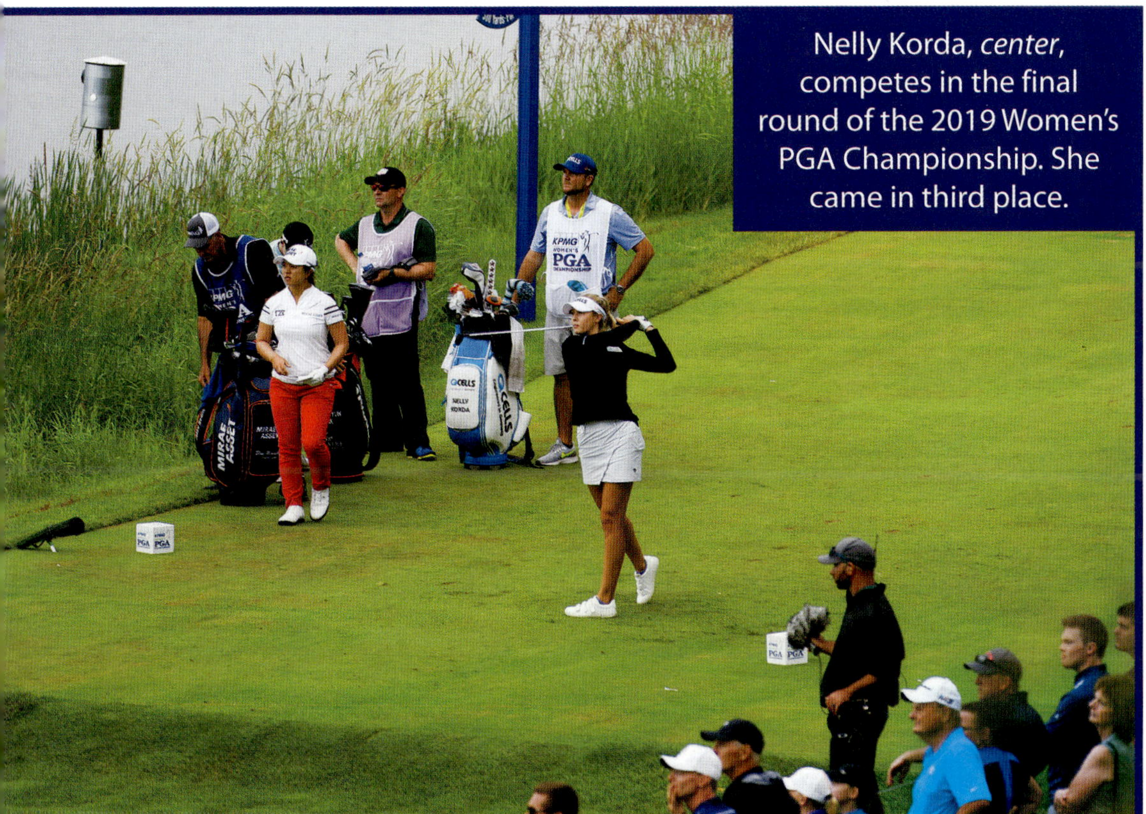

Nelly Korda, *center*, competes in the final round of the 2019 Women's PGA Championship. She came in third place.

SPECIAL TOURNAMENTS

Throughout the season, there are some events with different formats from traditional tournaments. In pro-am tournaments, professional golfers play with amateurs. One popular men's pro-am event is the AT&T Pebble Beach Pro-Am. Other tournaments are based on age. The PGA Tour Champions, for example, is for golfers ages 50 and up.

Match play events determine winners by the number of holes they win rather than by cumulative stroke scores. The lowest score on a hole wins the point. If there is a tie, the point is halved. The match ends when a player wins more holes than there are remaining to be played.

Match play is sometimes done in teams. These formats are usually four-ball or foursomes. Four-ball means each player

In the Pebble Beach Pro-Am, each pro golfer is matched up with a celebrity partner. Famous actor Bill Murray is a frequent participant at the event.

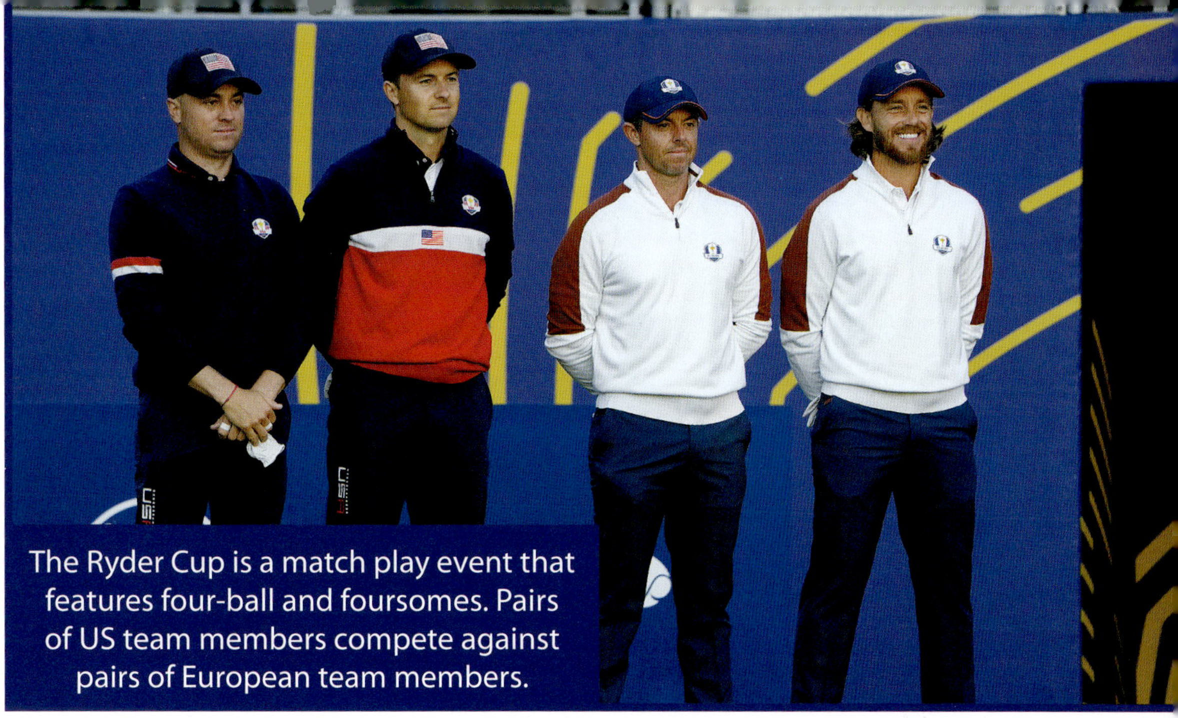

The Ryder Cup is a match play event that features four-ball and foursomes. Pairs of US team members compete against pairs of European team members.

on a two-person team plays their own ball through the hole. The lowest score between the pair is the team's score. In foursomes, only one ball is in play per team. Teammates take turns until they hole out, with the lowest score between teams winning the hole. The players take turns teeing off. One player hits first on odd-numbered holes, while the other hits first on even ones.

SCORING TERMS

Golf involves several scoring terms. *Par* means the expected number of strokes a golfer can make on a particular hole. On a par-4 hole, golfers are expected to take four strokes. If the golfer gets their ball in the hole in one shot, they make a *hole in one*. If they take one fewer stroke than the hole's par, they make a *birdie*. If the golfer takes one more stroke than the hole's par, they make a *bogey*. A double bogey happens when the golfer goes two strokes over par. If the golfer makes the hole in two strokes under par, it's an *eagle*.

THE MAJORS

In 2024, Augusta National hosted the 88th Masters Tournament. Scottie Scheffler, *center right*, won the tournament.

THE MASTERS

In 1933, amateur golfer Bobby Jones and investment banker Clifford Roberts founded Augusta National Golf Club in Georgia. In 1934, they started hosting the Augusta National Invitation Tournament. They changed its name to the Masters Tournament in 1939. In 1940, they started holding it during the first full week in April.

To play in the Masters, golfers must qualify or be invited by the Masters Committee. Players can qualify by winning or ranking in the top scores of other majors or PGA Tour tournaments. Previous Masters winners receive lifetime invitations.

TRADITIONS

The Masters is the most famous golf event. The winner receives a trophy and an iconic green jacket. In 1937, Augusta National members began wearing green jackets so fans would recognize them. In 1949, they began the tradition of giving a green jacket to the Masters champion. Winner Sam Snead was the first to receive one.

PAR 3 CONTEST

Masters week begins with the Par 3 Contest. This warm-up match happens before the first round of the tournament on a nine-hole course. Many players invite their families to be caddies or try making shots. Sam Snead won the first Par 3 Contest in 1960. However, winning the Par 3 Contest hasn't guaranteed success in the actual tournament. No player has won both events in the same year.

Another Masters tradition is the Champions Dinner. This is held before the tournament begins. Ben Hogan hosted the first dinner in 1952. Only prior Masters champions can attend. The defending champion chooses the menu. It often includes foods from his home state or country.

In 2015, 21-year-old Jordan Spieth won the Masters. The tournament's previous winner, Bubba Watson, presented Spieth with a green jacket.

Since 1940, caddies at the Masters have worn white coveralls. Professionals at the Masters were assigned caddies from Augusta National. This was different because at the time, most players had their own caddies who traveled with them. It wasn't until 1983 that players could use their own caddies for the Masters.

During the Masters, each caddie's jumpsuit has the name and number of their assigned golfer Velcroed onto it. The caddies also wear green ball caps.

Many standard tournament practices started at the Masters.

There are 11 scoreboards at Augusta National. During the Masters, volunteers update the scores by hand.

For example, Roberts changed the locations of perimeter mounds to improve gallery viewing. He also placed scoreboards throughout the course. Roberts came up with the idea of using red numbers for under par, a green zero for par, and green numbers for over par.

Arnold Palmer, *right*, won his fourth Masters Tournament in 1964. Jack Nicklaus presented him with a green jacket.

WINNERS

Arnold Palmer was the first to win four Masters. He was also the first to compete in 50 consecutive Masters. Gary Player eventually surpassed that mark, competing in 52 consecutive Masters. Through 2023, only eight golfers have won the Masters at least three times. Nine players have won twice.

No one has won more green jackets than Jack Nicklaus. He won six titles, claiming his first in 1963. Nicklaus was 46 years old when he won his last Masters in 1986, making him the oldest champion in the tournament's history.

Tiger Woods has won five green jackets. His first win in 1997 showcased his skill. Woods set 20 Masters records during the tournament, including the scoring record at 18 under par. He also set the record for largest margin of victory at 12 strokes. As of 2024, Woods remains the youngest champion in the tournament's history.

Jack Nicklaus, *bottom left*, was only 23 years old when he won the 1963 Masters. Between 1962 and 1966, Nicklaus and Arnold Palmer were the only two players to win the tournament.

CHEVRON CHAMPIONSHIP

The Chevron Championship tournament began in 1972, becoming a major in 1983. It is the first major on the LPGA's annual schedule. The tournament was founded by celebrity Dinah Shore and David Foster, the president of company Colgate-Palmolive. Shore was a strong advocate for women's golf who frequently promoted the LPGA Tour. She wanted to start a tournament to support the LPGA.

The tournament was originally called the Colgate-Dinah Shore Winner's Circle. In the 2020s, its name changed to the Chevron Championship after its lead sponsor Chevron, an energy company. The Chevron Championship trophy is called the Dinah Shore Trophy. This prize was created in the early 1980s.

TV personality Dinah Shore was closely involved in the Chevron Championship up until her death in 1994. She was the first nonplaying member of the LPGA Hall of Fame.

The first tournament was held at the Mission Hills Country Club in California. The course was eventually named the Dinah Shore Tournament Course. Over the years, the tournament has had many different title sponsors. But most people called it "the Dinah." It also became more than just a golf event. It featured events throughout the week that attracted celebrities and business moguls. The tournament has sometimes been called the Masters of women's golf. Like the Masters, it is the first major of the year and is played on the same course every year with a small, elite field.

A statue of Dinah Shore stands near the eighteenth hole of the Dinah Shore Tournament Course at Mission Hills Country Club.

TRADITIONS AND WINNERS

One Chevron Championship tradition is for winners to celebrate by jumping into the pond off the eighteenth green. This tradition began in 1988 when Amy Alcott made the leap and pulled her caddie in with her. She did it again three years later, taking Dinah Shore in with her. For more than 30 years, winners made the leap into Poppie's Pond. This name honors former tournament director Terry Wilcox. His grandchildren called him Poppie.

Amy Alcott, *left*, won the 1988 Chevron Championship by two strokes. It was her second time winning the tournament.

Angel Yin hits a shot from a bunker on the seventeenth hole during the final round of the 2023 Chevron Championship.

For 51 years, the Chevron Championship took place every March at the Dinah Shore Tournament Course. In 2023, the event found a new home and date. It's now held at the Club at Carlton Woods in The Woodlands, which is near Houston, Texas. The event is also held in April instead of March. These changes happened for several reasons. Chevron wanted to move the tournament and promised to increase the tournament purse from $3.1 million to $5 million. Moving the event to April also took it out of the shadow of other women's golf events scheduled in March.

2023 Chevron Championship winner Lilia Vu, *left*, jumps off the dock into the pond with LPGA physiotherapist Anne-Lise Bidou.

With the tournament at a new location, people wondered if the tradition of winners jumping into the water would continue. The eighteenth hole at the Club at Carlton Woods has a pond next to it, and preparations were made should the tradition continue. In 2023, Californian Lilia Vu won the tournament and leaped into the pond. The tournament has continued to pay tribute to its roots in other ways too. Winners still receive the Dinah Shore Trophy, and the hospitality area around the eighteenth green is called Dinah's Place.

Chevron Championship winners are given a white bathrobe to wear after they jump into the pond. Lilia Vu wore her robe while accepting the Dinah Shore Trophy.

MEN'S PGA CHAMPIONSHIP

The PGA Championship began in 1916. It is the only major that does not invite amateurs. Players must be members of the PGA of America to participate. A total of 156 players compete. During its first 41 years, it was a match play event. The PGA switched to stroke play after losing money in the 1957 event. It has followed that format ever since.

Unlike some other majors, the PGA Championship is not played on the same course every year. Several courses have

Rory McIlroy won his second PGA Championship in 2014. The tournament was held at Valhalla Golf Club that year.

Xander Schauffele celebrates after winning the 2024 PGA Championship at Valhalla Golf Club.

hosted it multiple times. Valhalla Golf Club in Louisville, Kentucky, and Oak Hill Country Club in Rochester, New York, have each hosted the PGA Championship four times. Southern Hills Country Club in Tulsa, Oklahoma, has hosted it five times.

The dates of the PGA Championship have also moved around. For a long time, the tournament took place in August and was the final major on the PGA Tour schedule. But Tour officials decided having the FedEx Cup playoffs in September wasn't a good thing. Football season started at the same time, making it hard to compete for viewers. They moved the playoffs to August, making it necessary to move other tournament dates. In 2019, the PGA Championship officially moved to May.

Jack Nicklaus speaks to the crowd after winning his fifth PGA Championship in 1980.

WINNERS AND RECORDS

The winner of the PGA Championship receives the Wanamaker Trophy. This prize is named after Rodman Wanamaker, who helped establish the first pro golf association. Walter Hagen and Jack Nicklaus have each won the PGA Championship five times. Hagen won it five times between 1921 and 1927. Four of his wins were consecutive.

Hagen was also the first to lose the trophy. When his string of victories ended in 1928, he revealed he had misplaced the trophy. It was discovered two years later in a leather case at a sporting goods warehouse in Detroit, Michigan.

Tiger Woods is one of two golfers to win back-to-back PGA Championships since 1958. He did so twice, in 1999 and 2000 and in 2006 and 2007. Brooks Koepka won in 2018 and 2019.

Tiger Woods hits a shot out of a bunker during the 2002 PGA Championship. Even though he came in second place, Woods considered it the best shot of his career.

There have been many memorable wins in PGA Championship history. John Daly was a little-known player who won the 1991 event. He wasn't even part of the original field. Daly was the ninth alternate, meaning nine original members of the field had to drop out before he would be invited. But nine players did drop out, so Daly traveled from more than 500 miles (800 km) away to participate in the tournament. His long drives and daring play caught the crowd's attention, and Daly became a star.

John Daly was 25 years old when he won the 1991 PGA Championship at Crooked Stick Golf Club in Indiana. He won by three strokes.

Although Arnold Palmer never won a PGA Championship, he came in second place in the 1964, 1968, and 1970 tournaments.

There's a surprising name among those who have never won the PGA Championship. Arnold Palmer played in the event 37 times, more than any other player. He finished in second place three times during his career. It was the only major he didn't win, leaving him one shy of a career grand slam.

The 2019 Women's PGA Championship was held at Hazeltine National Golf Club in Minnesota. Australian Hannah Green, *center*, won the tournament.

WOMEN'S PGA CHAMPIONSHIP

The Women's PGA Championship is the major that is the second-longest running on the LPGA Tour. It began in 1955 at Orchard Ridge Country Club in Indiana. It was called the LPGA Championship. It was the only time the event ended with a match play final round after three rounds of stroke play. In 1956, the event switched to four stroke-play rounds.

During its first six years, the championship took place at four different courses. Afterward, it had long-term host sites. Two courses have hosted the event 11 times. Ohio's Jack Nicklaus Sports Center hosted it from 1978 to 1988, while Delaware's DuPont Country Club hosted it from 1994 to 2004. In 2014, the event began changing courses every year. This way, the event could be held at courses that were typically affiliated with men's tournaments.

Mariah Stackhouse hits a shot during the 2023 Women's PGA Championship at Baltusrol Golf Club.

In 2015, the LPGA gave the PGA control of the event. This way, it would have access to the PGA's resources, including a bigger prize fund, better television coverage, and access to courses. The tournament purse grew from $2.25 million in 2014 to $10 million in 2023.

The championship has a field of 156 players. Golfers who aren't on the LPGA Tour can participate, but they must be PGA/LPGA club professionals. They must also qualify based on their performance in the Women's Stroke Play Championship, which happens the year before the major.

WINNERS AND RECORDS

Mickey Wright dominated the Women's PGA Championship in its early years, winning four times between 1958 and 1963. As of 2023, she is the only four-time winner. Kathy Whitworth, Nancy Lopez, Annika Sörenstam, Se Ri Pak, and Inbee Park have each won three times. Sörenstam and Park are the only players to win three consecutive times.

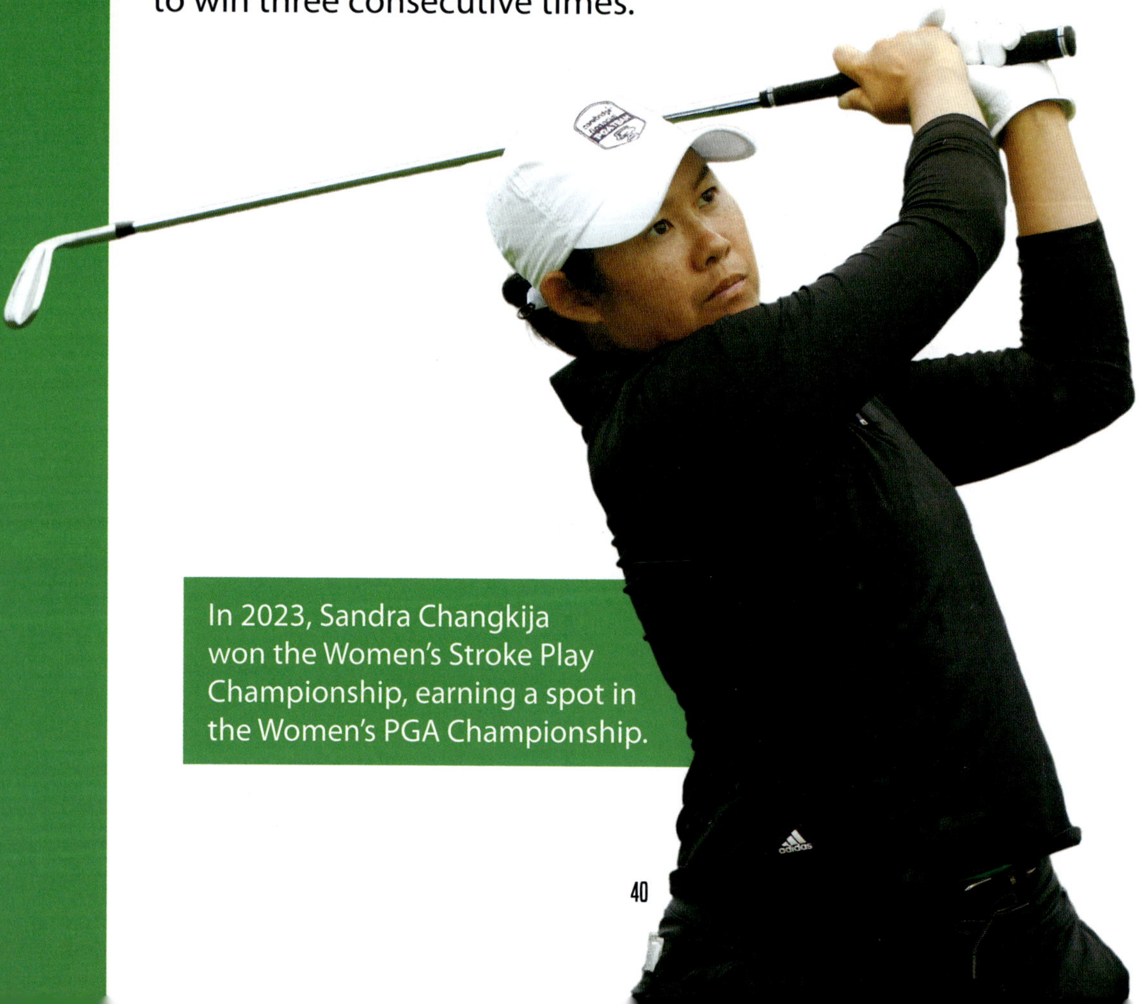

In 2023, Sandra Changkija won the Women's Stroke Play Championship, earning a spot in the Women's PGA Championship.

Mickey Wright won the Women's PGA Championship in 1958, 1960, 1961, and 1963.

The tournament record for most strokes under par is 19. Cristie Kerr was the first to achieve this in 2010. Her feat was matched by Yani Tseng in 2011, Inbee Park in 2015, and Nelly Korda in 2021. In Kerr's 2010 victory, she also set the record for largest margin of victory at 12 strokes.

Inbee Park celebrates her 2015 Women's PGA Championship victory with her husband, Gi Hyeob Nam.

After Sei Young Kim's 2020 win, she held several Women's PGA Championship records. Her four-round total of 266 broke Betsy King's 28-year-old record of 267. Kim's victory was partially due to her record low of 63 in the final round.

HOLE IN ONE

Three times in Women's PGA Championship history, there have been two holes in one in the same year. This first happened in 1974, when Jane Blalock and Bonnie Bryant made holes in one at Pleasant Valley Country Club. Rosie Jones and Gloria Park did it in 2001 at DuPont Country Club. In 2018, Brittany Marchand and Lexi Thompson achieved the feat at Kemper Lakes Golf Club.

She became the fifth golfer to shoot a 63 at the Women's PGA Championship, but she was the first to do so in the final round. In 2016, 18-year-old Canadian Brooke Henderson became the tournament's youngest winner.

Winner Sei Young Kim poses with the Women's PGA Championship trophy in 2020. The victory made Kim the eighteenth South Korean golfer to win a major.

US OPEN

First played in 1895, the US Open is the second-longest-running major. It takes place every June, and 156 male professionals and amateurs participate. However, they must first qualify. A player's Handicap Index, or the calculated number representing their scoring ability, cannot exceed a certain number. In 2024, that number was 0.4. Players can also make the field by winning qualifying tournaments.

The crowd watches Bobby Jones take a shot during the 1929 US Open at Winged Foot Golf Club. Jones went on to win the tournament.

Wyndham Clark celebrates a putt during the 2023 US Open at the Los Angeles Country Club. Clark won the tournament.

The US Open course changes every year. The course is designed to test golfers' skills. The courses are usually long, with narrow fairways and areas of rough. Sometimes par-5 holes are marked par 4s during the US Open. Because of this, several winners have finished over par.

1913 US Open winner Francis Ouimet, *center*, poses for a photograph with Harry Vardon, *left*, and Ted Ray, *right*.

WINNERS AND RECORDS

The US Open holds a prestigious place in the golf world. But the tournament had humble beginnings. The first US Open had 11 players and was held at Rhode Island's Newport Golf and Country Club. Participants played 36 holes in one day, and Horace Rawlins won. His prize was $150 and a gold medal. Rawlins also got to keep the US Open trophy for one year.

In 1911, 19-year-old John McDermott became the first American and youngest player to win the US Open. The tournament gained national attention in 1913, when Francis Ouimet became the first amateur to win. He beat world-famous players Harry Vardon and Ted Ray.

A famous golf photo was taken at Merion Golf Club during the 1950 US Open. It shows Ben Hogan hitting a 1 iron, a notoriously difficult club, onto the green before making par to force a playoff. It was Hogan's first tournament since being in a car crash the previous year. Hogan made the par and won the 18-hole playoff the following day. The victory became known as the Miracle at Merion.

WOODS AT THE US OPEN

In 2008, Tiger Woods had one of the best US Open performances. The win was remarkable because Woods competed with a broken leg. Before the tournament, he had suffered a stress fracture while recovering from knee surgery. He played four rounds, an 18-hole playoff, and a sudden death hole before finally winning.

At Merion Golf Club, a plaque marks the spot where Ben Hogan made his famous shot during the 1950 US Open.

In 1960, Arnold Palmer was seven strokes behind the leader in the final round of the US Open at Colorado's Cherry Hills Country Club. Palmer got birdies on six of the first seven holes. It was enough to win. Jack Nicklaus, playing as an amateur, came in second. But Nicklaus went on to defeat Palmer in the 1962 US Open. It was the first of Nicklaus's four tournament wins. He tied for the most wins in US Open history, alongside Willie Anderson, Ben Hogan, and Bobby Jones.

Arnold Palmer, *second from left*, and Jack Nicklaus, *right*, smile after tying for first place in the 1962 US Open. Nicklaus would later defeat Palmer in a playoff.

Rory McIlroy was 22 years old when he won the 2011 US Open.

In 2011, Rory McIlroy had a record-setting performance at the US Open. He won with a 16-under 268, setting the record for lowest 72-hole score in the tournament's history. It was one of 12 US Open records that McIlroy set or tied that year.

Patty Berg, *center*, competed in the US Women's Open several times during her career. But she won the tournament only once, in 1946.

US WOMEN'S OPEN

The US Women's Open is the longest-standing women's golf major, but it wasn't a major until 1950. The tournament is open to both amateurs and professionals. Their Handicap Index cannot exceed a certain number, and they must qualify over 36 holes at various courses if they aren't already part of the field.

The first US Women's Open took place in 1946 at Spokane Country Club in Washington State. Only six of 32 competitors were professionals. Patty Berg won, taking home $5,600 in war bonds. It was the only match play US Women's Open. Over time, more professionals participated. In 1969, 70 of the 99 participants were professionals.

Many amateurs participated in the tournament's early years, but only one nonprofessional has won.

Amateur Catherine Lacoste took home the trophy in 1967. Nine other amateurs have tied for or finished in second place.

In 1976, there were too many entries to include everyone. Because of this, the US Women's Open began holding qualifying tournaments. The entries continued growing. By 2004, 1,000 players entered. By 2023, that number jumped to more than 2,000.

The US Women's Open is held at different locations each year. In 2023, the tournament took place at Pebble Beach Golf Links in California.

WINNERS AND RECORDS

Some of the greatest female golfers have been US Women's Open champions. The 1948 US Women's Open was the first of three that Babe Didrikson Zaharias won. In 1959, Mickey Wright became the first to win back-to-back US Women's Opens. She went on to win four titles. She and Betsy Rawls are the only players to do so. Didrikson Zaharias, Susie Maxwell Berning, Hollis Stacy, and Annika Sörenstam have all won three times.

Mickey Wright holds the Harton S. Semple Trophy after winning her third US Women's Open title in 1961.

PRIZE MONEY

Prize money for the US Women's Open has changed greatly over the years. In 1974, winner Sandra Haynie earned $6,031. The total purse that year was $40,000. Four years later, the purse more than doubled to $100,000. In 1990, the total prize money was $500,000. By 2000, that was the winner's prize. The 2019 winner received a seven-figure payout, making Jeongeun Lee6 the first million-dollar US Women's Open champion.

Annika Sörenstam hits a shot from a sand trap at the 1996 US Women's Open.

Sörenstam's 1995 US Women's Open title was also her first pro title. She started the final round five strokes behind, but she had birdies on holes 9, 10, and 11. She shot a final-round 68 to win. Sörenstam also won the 1996 tournament, becoming the sixth player to win it in consecutive years.

The first international winner was Uruguay's Fay Crocker in 1955. American players dominated the tournament until Sörenstam's 1995 victory. From 1995 to 2022, international players won 20 of the tournament's 28 events.

South Korean Se Ri Pak won the 1998 US Women's Open. At 20 years old, she was the youngest winner ever at the time.

Se Ri Pak celebrates after winning the 1998 US Women's Open in a 20-hole playoff. She was the first Korean golfer to win the tournament.

Hawaiian Allisen Corpuz won the 2023 US Women's Open. It was her first LPGA Tour victory.

In the playoff round, she took off her shoes and socks to stand in the water and hit a shot out of the rough. She helped set off a golf revolution in Korea. Between her 1998 win and the 2020 US Women's Open, ten Korean golfers won the title.

James Braid, *center*, was photographed competing in the 1908 British Open. That year, he won the tournament by eight strokes.

BRITISH OPEN

The Open Championship, known as the British Open, began in 1860. It started after Scottish golfer Allan Robertson died in 1859. Prestwick Golf Club members started a contest to determine the new Champion Golfer of the Year. They organized the first British Open.

During the tournament's first 29 years, Scottish players won the title of Champion Golfer and the Claret Jug trophy. Old Tom Morris and his son Young Tom Morris won eight of the first thirteen tournaments. James Braid became the first five-time champion in 1910. Braid, Harry Vardon, and J. H. Taylor each held five British Open titles until Vardon won his sixth in 1914.

Professionals and amateurs must qualify to participate in the British Open. Players do so by winning or ranking in the top scores of qualifying events. Players who have won previous British Opens or other majors do not have to qualify. The tournament is famous for being played on links-style courses, or courses on sandy, rugged land with hazards such as dunes.

Australian Cameron Smith, *right*, shakes hands with caddie Sam Pinfold during the 2022 British Open. Smith won the tournament.

WINNERS

In 1890, Englishman John Ball became the first non-Scot to win the British Open. Forty-one years later, Jock Hutchison became the first US citizen to win in 1921. Hutchison was born in Scotland but had become a US citizen. One year later, Walter Hagen became the first American-born winner. He won three more times during the 1920s. US players won 11 of the

Walter Hagen, *left*, walks with his caddie, Jimmy McDonald, during a British Open practice round in 1926.

After winning the 1961 British Open, Arnold Palmer poses with the Claret Jug trophy at Royal Birkdale Golf Club.

13 tournaments between 1921 and 1933. Through 2023, 31 Americans have won, the most of any nation.

After World War II (1939–1945), few Americans participated in the British Open. But in 1960, Arnold Palmer hoped to grab his third major victory of the year and complete a grand slam. Palmer lost, but he later won the 1961 and 1962 Claret Jugs. His success made the British Open more relevant to Americans.

Tom Watson won his third British Open at Muirfield in 1980.

The British Open's greatest American winner was Tom Watson. He first won in 1975 and went on to win the event four more times. In 2009, 59-year-old Watson almost became the tournament's oldest champion, but he finished second.

Between 1970 and 1983, Americans won the Claret Jug 12 times. US golfers experienced another hot streak from 1995 to 2006. Tiger Woods won three British Opens, while other Americans won seven more times.

DUEL IN THE SUN

At the 1977 British Open, Tom Watson competed against Jack Nicklaus. They were tied for most of the tournament. Watson pulled a stroke ahead on hole 17. On the eighteenth hole, Nicklaus hit his drive into the rough. Watson was on the green in two, meaning Nicklaus had to get on the green from his difficult position and then make one putt. He succeeded, forcing Watson to make his putt to win. Watson did, shooting the lowest winning score in British Open history at 12 under par. Because Turnberry Golf Course had dried out that summer, the showdown became known as the Duel in the Sun.

In 2023, Brian Harman won the British Open. He became the fifteenth American to win the tournament in 20 years.

WOMEN'S OPEN

The first Women's Open was held in 1976, 116 years after the men's British Open began. The women's tournament struggled to gain a footing. It wasn't until 1994 that it became a regular LPGA stop. It would take another seven years before the event was recognized as a major. After that, the Women's Open was more commonly held at courses typically used for men's tournaments.

Jenny Lee Smith was an amateur when she won the first Women's Open in 1976. She turned pro the next year.

The Women's Open evolved from the Ladies Amateur Stroke Play Championship when professional players were added to the field in 1976. England's Jenny Lee Smith was the first winner. English players have won eight times as of 2023, the second most for any country. The only Scottish player to win the Women's Open was Catriona Matthew in 2009. South Korean golfers have won the event six times since 2001, when Se Ri Pak took home her first Women's Open title. Golfers from 13 different countries have won, with the United States claiming the most victories.

Charley Hull hits a shot during the 2023 Women's Open. That year, the tournament was held at Walton Heath Golf Club in England.

WINNERS AND RECORDS

US players won the title 12 times during the first 47 years of the Women's Open. In 1980, Debbie Massey became the first American winner. In 1981, she became the first to win the event in back-to-back years.

American Sherri Steinhauer also won in back-to-back years, claiming her first victory in 1998. She became the second three-time Women's Open winner in 2006. She was also the oldest winner at age 43.

Sherri Steinhauer takes a shot during the 2006 Women's Open. She went on to win by three strokes.

Alongside Steinhauer, Karrie Webb is the only other three-time Women's Open winner. In 1995, 20-year-old Webb won her first Women's Open. She closed out her third round with an eagle. Then she started her fourth round with four birdies on the first ten holes. This led to a six-stroke win over Annika Sörenstam and Jill McGill.

Two years later, Webb followed that win with a scoring record of 19 under par and a total score of 269 for an eight-stroke victory. However, when Webb won, the Women's Open wasn't a major yet. To complete her career grand slam, Webb had to win the event again. She did so in 2002, just one year after the tournament achieved major status.

Jiyai Shin and Yani Tseng are also two-time winners. Shin's 2008 win made her the youngest Women's Open winner at 20 years old. In 2012, she won a second time by nine strokes, the largest margin of victory in the major era. Tseng won her first Women's Open in 2010. When she won her second Women's Open in 2011, she became the youngest golfer ever to win five majors.

Karrie Webb celebrates after winning the 2002 Women's Open at Turnberry Golf Club. It was the sixth major of her career.

Since 1979, the tournament has awarded the Smyth Salver to the lowest-scoring amateur who completes the 72-hole tournament. Former winners have gone on to have great professional careers. They include Michelle Wie West, Anna Nordqvist, Lydia Ko, Danielle Kang, and Georgia Hall. Hall won the 2018 Women's Open five years after winning the Smyth Salver.

Michelle Wie West has competed in the Women's Open as both an amateur and a professional. In the 2012 tournament, she tied for thirteenth place.

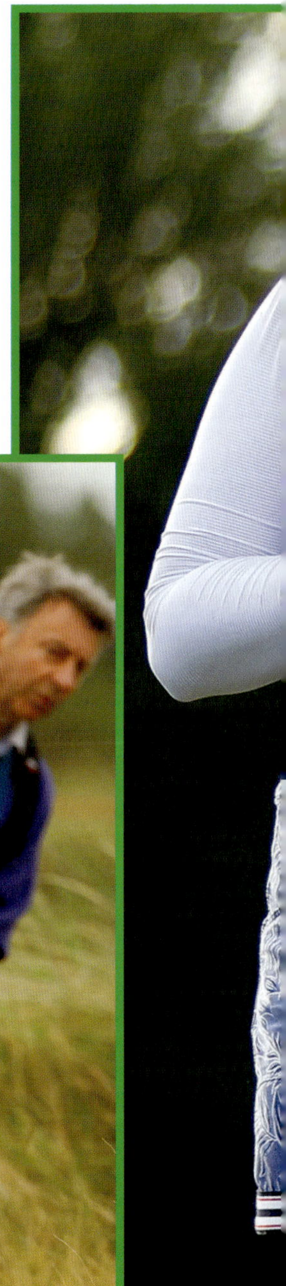

2023 Women's Open winner Lilia Vu, *left*, and Smyth Salver winner Charlotte Heath, *right*, pose for a photo together.

EVIAN CHAMPIONSHIP

The Evian Championship is the youngest of the five LPGA Tour majors. It is also the only major held in continental Europe. The tournament began in 1994 as the Evian Masters, an LET event. In 2000,

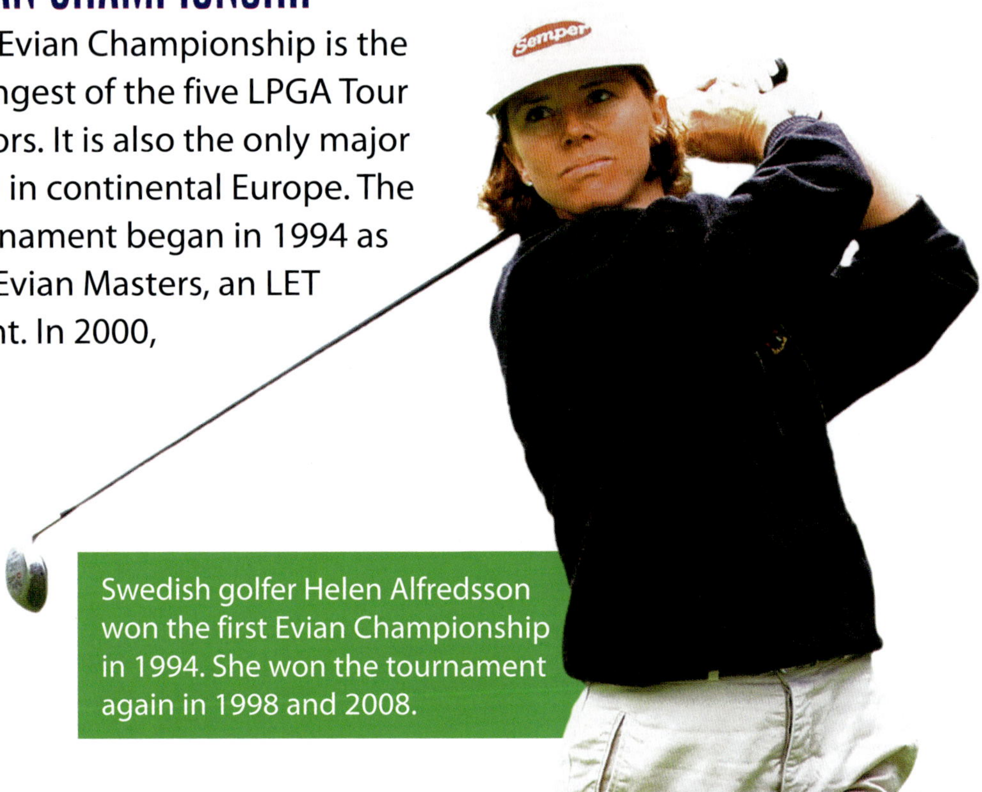

Swedish golfer Helen Alfredsson won the first Evian Championship in 1994. She won the tournament again in 1998 and 2008.

FIFTH MAJOR

The LPGA's addition of a fifth major created controversy. People wondered about players who had achieved a career grand slam before a fifth major was added. They worried those players' accomplishments would no longer be recognized. This was worrisome for retired golfers who wouldn't have a chance to win the fifth major. The LPGA decided that those who had won each of the four majors before the addition of the Evian Championship would still be recognized as having career grand slams. Players who had won the previous four in addition to the newest major would have a Super Career Grand Slam.

the LPGA added the competition to its list of events. As a nod to international golfers on the LPGA Tour, the event was made a fifth major in 2013.

The Evian Championship is the final major held every year. It was originally played in September, but poor weather led to shortened tournaments in 2013 and 2017. In 2017, the playoff holes happened in a sleet storm. Officials later announced that the 2018 tournament would be the last one in September. The tournament moved to July. The Evian Championship is the only women's major that has been held at the same course every year. It takes place at Evian Resort Golf Club in France, near Lake Geneva.

The Evian Championship takes place on the Evian Resort Golf Club's Champions Course. It opened in 1904 and was redesigned in the 1980s.

A skydiver descends with a parachute and a French flag during the 2023 Evian Championship trophy presentation ceremony.

When the tournament was called the Evian Masters, it was known for its post-tournament celebrations. Some celebrations stopped when the tournament became a major, but the event still has some flourishes. For example, a skydiver delivers the trophy with a flag representing the winner's home country.

WINNERS AND RECORDS

Before the Evian Championship became a major, Helen Alfredsson won it three times. During the event's first ten years as a major, there were ten different winners. The first was Suzann Pettersen, who finished two shots ahead of 16-year-old amateur Lydia Ko. Two years later, Ko became the youngest player to win a women's major, winning the 2015 Evian Championship at age 18.

New Zealander Lydia Ko defeated American Lexi Thompson to win the 2015 Evian Championship. She won by six strokes.

In 2021, Minjee Lee came from seven strokes back at the start of the final round. She shot a seven-under 64, ending up in a playoff with Jeongeun Lee6. On the first playoff hole, Lee put her second shot near the hole for a potential eagle. Lee6 missed the green, ending up in the water on her second shot. This meant Lee could take two putts to win. It was Lee's first time winning a major.

Jeongeun Lee6 takes a shot during the 2021 Evian Championship. She added the number 6 to her last name to help distinguish herself from five other golfers with the same name.

In 2023, Céline Boutier won the Evian Championship. She became the third French woman to win a major. The first two were Catherine Lacoste and Patricia Meunier-Lebouc.

In 2023, Céline Boutier became the first Frenchwoman to win the Evian Championship.

TEAM GOLF TOURNAMENTS

RYDER CUP

The Ryder Cup is a biennial match between a US men's golf team and a European men's golf team. The event rotates between European and American courses. Each team has 12 golfers. Some qualify for the team based on their rankings in other events, while others are chosen by team captains. The captain is not always a player on the team.

Team captain Walter Hagen accepts the Ryder Cup after the US team's victory in 1937.

At the 1991 Ryder Cup, Americans Steve Pate, *left*, and Corey Pavin, *second from left*, competed in a four-ball match against Europeans Bernhard Langer, *third from left*, and Colin Montgomerie, *right*.

The tournament lasts three days. On the first two days, teams play one four-match session of four-ball and one four-match session of foursomes. The final day involves singles. Each match is worth one point, and 28 points are available. Teams must earn at least 14.5 points to win. If teams tie, the Cup stays with the previous event's winner.

The first Ryder Cup was held in 1927 at Worcester Country Club in Massachusetts. Great Britain played against the United States. In 1973, Ireland joined the British squad. In 1979, the team expanded to include continental Europe.

The US team dominated the first 25 Ryder Cups, winning 22 times, including 13 consecutive times. In 1985, the European team earned its first win in 28 years. The Europeans had

Fans cheer during the 2023 Ryder Cup at Marco Simone Golf and Country Club in Rome, Italy. More than 271,000 people attended the event.

their first win on US soil at Ohio's Muirfield Village Golf Club in 1987. Europe also dominated the Ryder Cup in the early 2000s, winning six of the first seven matches. Europe won its fourteenth Ryder Cup in 2023. At that time, the United States had 27 wins.

A UNIQUE TOURNAMENT

The Ryder Cup is popular due to its exciting matches. Fans also enjoy rooting for teams. There have been many contentious moments in the tournament. Sometimes bad blood was born from gamesmanship, such as captains ordering irons to be examined.

In the 1991 "War by the Shore" match, the Americans shook off a losing streak when Europe missed a short par putt that

would have won them the final match. American fans exploded with joy. In 1999, the Americans mounted a comeback. Justin Leonard sank a long putt on hole 17, clinching the half point the Americans needed. The crowd stormed the green. But Europe's José María Olazábal still had to putt.

Luke Donald, *center*, served as captain of the 2023 European Ryder Cup team. The team defeated the US team 16.5–11.5.

PRESIDENTS CUP

The Presidents Cup pits a US men's team against a team of international players from outside Europe. The event began in 1994 and is held in years between the Ryder Cup. The host site alternates between US and overseas venues. Each team has 12 golfers. Some qualify based on their rankings, while others are captain's picks. The event lasts four days and includes 30 total points.

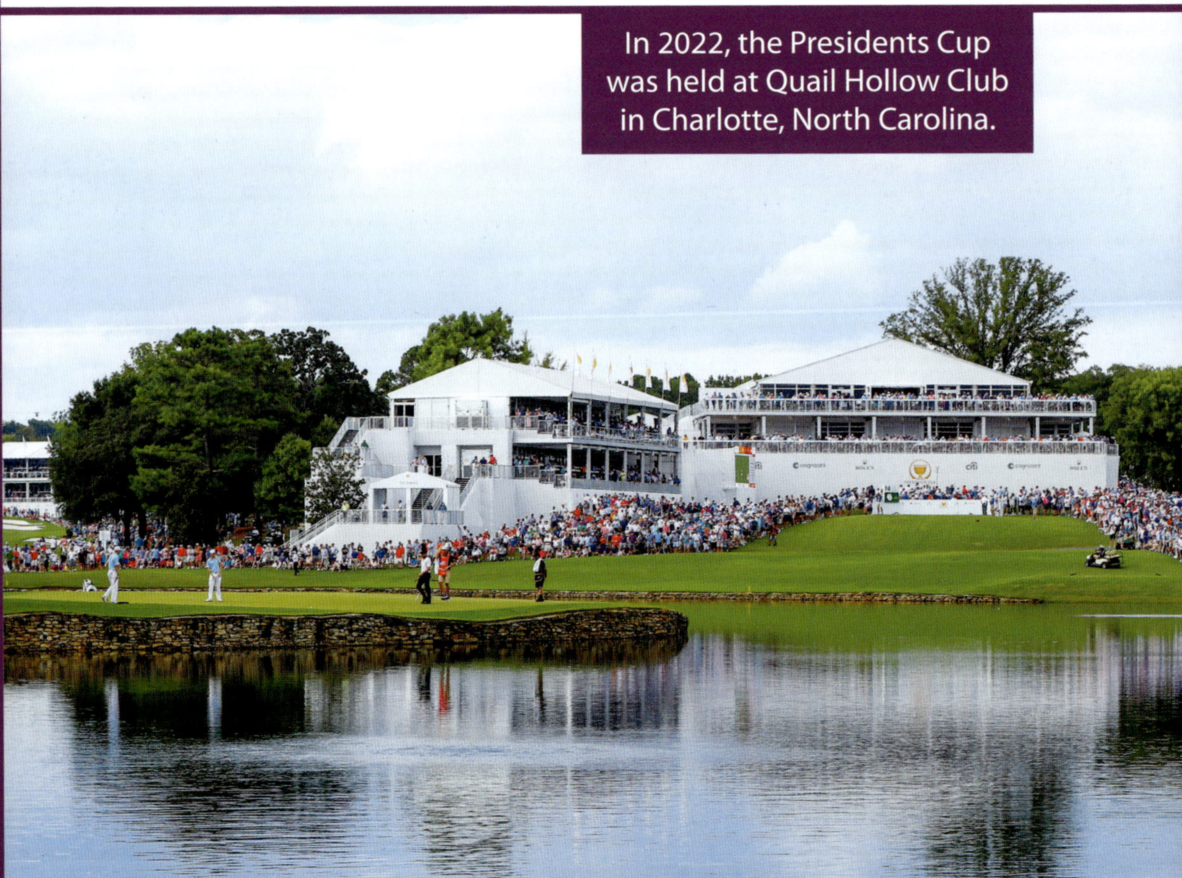

In 2022, the Presidents Cup was held at Quail Hollow Club in Charlotte, North Carolina.

The US team won the 2022 Presidents Cup by a score of 17.5–12.5. Davis Love III, *holding trophy*, served as team captain.

On each of the first two days, five matches take place. These are either four-ball or foursomes. Those who play four-ball on the first day play foursomes on the second day, and vice versa. The third day features eight matches, with four-ball and foursomes split between the morning and afternoon. The final day features 12 singles matches. The lowest score on each hole gets a point, while ties are half a point. The winner of each match earns a point.

The United States won the first two Presidents Cups, while the international team won in 1998. The United States won again in 2000, with the first tie happening in 2003. The US team won nine straight times after the tie, including in 2022.

Team captain JoAnne Carner holds the Solheim Cup after the US team won the tournament in 1994. The team won by a score of 13–7.

SOLHEIM CUP

The Solheim Cup began in 1990. It is a biennial match between a US women's golf team and a European women's golf team. Each team has 12 golfers, with US players from the LPGA and European players from the LET. The event alternates between US and European courses.

The Solheim Cup lasts three days. The first two days involve morning foursome matches and afternoon four-ball matches. The final day features singles. Each match is worth one point, and 28 points are available. Teams need at least 14.5 points to win. If teams tie, the Cup stays with the previous event's winner.

The crowd watches Georgia Hall compete for the European team during the 2019 Solheim Cup. That year, the tournament took place at Gleneagles in Scotland.

WINNERS AND RECORDS

The United States won four of the first five Solheim Cups. But as of 2023, each team has retained the Cup for three straight events at least once. In 2019, Suzann Pettersen sank the winning putt for Europe. It was her ninth appearance in the Solheim Cup, and she had made the team as a captain's pick. The teams were tied going into the final day and final match. Pettersen was tied with American Marina Alex when they teed off on the eighteenth hole. Then Pettersen made a seven-foot putt to win the match.

European team captain Suzann Pettersen celebrates during the 2023 Solheim Cup trophy presentation ceremony. It was the European team's eighth time winning the tournament.

US team member Alison Lee competes in a four-ball match during the 2015 Solheim Cup. She and Brittany Lincicome faced off against Europe's Suzann Pettersen and Charley Hull.

The United States had a big comeback in 2015. The Americans trailed 6–10 going into the final day and were upset with how one of the four-ball matches had ended. After American Alison Lee missed a putt on the seventeenth to win the hole, she picked up her ball. She thought she had heard the European team concede the putt. When a golfer concedes a putt, they allow their opponent to count the putt as made without getting the ball into the hole. But Pettersen said the putt hadn't been conceded. As a result, the US team lost the hole and match. But the team went on to win 8.5 points on the final day, securing the biggest comeback in Solheim history.

FAMOUS COURSES

The three holes of Amen Corner are named after plants that grow nearby. The twelfth hole, *pictured*, is called Golden Bell.

AUGUSTA NATIONAL

Augusta National is where the Masters takes place. Golfer Bobby Jones and investment banker Clifford Roberts founded the course. It was built in 1932 in Augusta, Georgia.

The course is known for holes 11, 12, and 13. In 1958, a writer dubbed this area "Amen Corner." Waterways weave through it. Players can risk hitting the ball into the hazard or choose to go for par.

Three bridges on the course commemorate historic Masters moments. Sarazen Bridge crosses the pond near the fifteenth hole. It marks where Gene Sarazen hit a famous shot in 1935. Hogan Bridge crosses Rae's Creek near the twelfth hole. It honors Ben Hogan's 1953 four-round score of 274. The third bridge commemorates Byron Nelson's 1937 Masters performance.

EISENHOWER

US president Dwight Eisenhower played at Augusta National. He suggested adding a pond, which was named Ike's Pond. The Eisenhower Cabin sits off the tenth tee. The Eisenhower Tree sat near the seventeenth hole. Eisenhower hit it so often that he asked for its removal. But the tree wasn't removed until 2014.

Sarazen Bridge is a flat footbridge made of stone. It was the first bridge at Augusta National to be dedicated to a golfer.

BETHPAGE BLACK

Bethpage Black is on Long Island, New York. It was the first publicly owned course to host the US Open. It first hosted in 2002, challenging players with its length, elevated greens, and heavy rough. The area's New York fans created a raucous atmosphere.

The course opened in 1936 as part of the building of Bethpage State Park. It is one of five courses in the park, all of which have color names. While the course became world famous in 2002, locals have long known about its attractions. A sign for the course says, "Warning—The Black Course is an

The fifteenth hole, *pictured*, is considered to have one of the toughest greens on the Bethpage Black course.

Brooks Koepka competes during the 2019 PGA Championship at Bethpage Black.

extremely difficult course which we recommend only for highly skilled golfers."

The 2002 US Open at Bethpage Black proved so challenging that only Tiger Woods finished under par. The course hosted the US Open again in 2009. Bethpage Black also hosted the 2019 PGA Championship and was scheduled to host the 2025 Ryder Cup.

Carnoustie features three golf courses, including the Championship Course. The course's eighteenth hole, *pictured*, is located by a hotel.

CARNOUSTIE

People have been golfing at Scotland's Carnoustie Golf Links since the 1500s. The Championship Course was laid out almost two centuries ago and is the world's oldest artisan golf club. Scottish golfer Allan Robertson designed the course. Today, his layout is still recognizable.

In 2019, Carnoustie was voted Best Golf Course in the World. It has hosted many prestigious men's and women's golf events. It has held the British Open, Women's Open, and Senior Open multiple times.

Each hole at Carnoustie has a name. The 1953 British Open inspired a name change for one of the holes. That year, Ben Hogan won the Claret Jug. His victory was due to the way he played the sixth hole. He took the high-risk, high-reward route by hitting his drive between the bunkers and the out-of-bounds line in each round. To commemorate Hogan's win, the hole was renamed Hogan's Alley in 2003.

The Carnoustie course is known for its challenging hazards, including 112 bunkers.

HAZELTINE

Hazeltine National Golf Club opened in 1962 in Chaska, Minnesota. The course hosted the US Women's Open four years after opening and again in 1977. Hazeltine hosted the 2019 Women's PGA Championship and was scheduled to host again in 2026.

In 1970, Hazeltine hosted the US Open. Tony Jacklin became

SIXTEENTH HOLE

Hazeltine's sixteenth hole is difficult. To reach the fairway, golfers must drive their ball over Hazeltine Lake but keep it short of the creek on the left side. The green is narrow and elevated. Golfer Johnny Miller called it the hardest par 4 he had ever played.

Hannah Green competes on Hazeltine's par-3 eighth hole during the 2019 Women's PGA Championship.

A photo of Arnold Palmer is displayed on a screen during the 2016 Ryder Cup at Hazeltine.

the first English winner in 46 years. His seven-stroke margin of victory was the largest since 1921. The US Open returned to Hazeltine in 1991.

The 2016 Ryder Cup at Hazeltine featured a remembrance for Arnold Palmer, who had died days earlier. The United States won 17–11. In 2029, Hazeltine was scheduled to become the first US venue to host the Ryder Cup a second time.

One of the Ocean Course's most difficult holes is the par-3 seventeenth hole, *pictured*. It includes bunkers and a large water hazard.

KIAWAH OCEAN COURSE

Kiawah Ocean Course is in Kiawah Island, South Carolina. It was chosen as the 1991 Ryder Cup site before there was a course there. Golf course architect Pete Dye designed it, using the area's Atlantic coastline and unpredictable winds to create one of the toughest US courses. It has the most seaside holes of any North American course.

The 1991 Ryder Cup was a major debut for the Ocean Course. The Americans won when Bernhard Langer missed a par putt that would have secured Europe's victory. The win broke the US team's losing streak.

In 1996, the Ocean Course hosted the Shell's Wonderful World of Golf match. It featured Annika Sörenstam and Dottie Pepper. It was the highest-rated edition of the show featuring two LPGA players.

The 2012 and 2021 PGA Championships took place at the Ocean Course. Rory McIlroy won in 2012 by eight strokes, the largest margin of victory in the PGA Championship. In 2021, Phil Mickelson won.

Phil Mickelson competes during the 2021 PGA Championship at the Ocean Course. He won the tournament by two strokes.

OAKMONT

Oakmont Country Club is outside Pittsburgh, Pennsylvania. Built in 1903, it gained attention after hosting the 1916 Intercollegiate National Championship. Oakmont has since become famous for hosting the US Open.

Oakmont first hosted the US Open in 1927. It was scheduled to host again in 2025, marking its tenth

American Andrew Landry competes in the 116th US Open at Oakmont in 2016.

Oakmont's Church Pews Bunker is made up of 12 rows and is about 100 yards (91 m) long.

time hosting. The tournament has happened at Oakmont at least once every decade since the 1950s. Oakmont has hosted PGA Championships, US Women's Opens, and amateur events.

Oakmont was originally a links course. But after someone called Oakmont ugly in 1953, officials planted trees. Decades later, they removed many of the trees. One of Oakmont's special features is the Church Pews Bunker between holes 3 and 4. It features grassy rows that look like pews.

VICTORIES

Dustin Johnson, Ernie Els, Johnny Miller, and Jack Nicklaus claimed their first major victories at Oakmont. Miller's final-round 63 was a major championship record score for more than four decades. Nicklaus defeated Arnold Palmer in Palmer's home state.

There are nine seaside holes on the Pebble Beach course, including the par-4 ninth hole, *pictured*.

PEBBLE BEACH

Pebble Beach is next to the Pacific Ocean on California's Monterey Peninsula. It has hosted several US Opens and the 2023 US Women's Open. The course was scheduled to host both events again throughout the 2030s and 2040s.

Pebble Beach gained fame at the 1929 US Amateur Championship. In 1972, it hosted its first US Open. At the 2000 US Open at Pebble Beach, Tiger Woods set or tied nine records.

Pebble Beach is used for the AT&T Pebble Beach Pro-Am, originally called Crosby National Pro-Am. Singer Bing Crosby

arranged a tournament for amateurs to play alongside professionals. Today, famous actors, singers, and athletes participate. Since 1977, both male and female amateurs have played in the event.

Pebble Beach's par-5 eighteenth hole is famous. The ocean borders it on the left, and a tree sits in the middle of the fairway. Golfers trying to reach the green in two shots can try driving the ball between the ocean and tree. Or they can hit to the right of the tree.

Pebble Beach's eighteenth hole, *pictured*, is considered one of the most famous finishing holes in golf. The site has also been voted the country's number-one public golf course.

PINEHURST NO. 2

Pinehurst No. 2 is in North Carolina. The course opened in 1907 and has hosted many events. In 2020, Pinehurst No. 2 was named the US Open's first anchor site. This meant it was selected to host every fifth US Open from 2024 through 2047.

The year 2024 marked the twenty-fifth anniversary of the 1999 US Open at Pinehurst No. 2. Phil Mickelson lost to

Pinehurst No. 2's par-4 second hole, *pictured*, is one of the most difficult holes on the course.

Payne Stewart, *bottom right*, celebrates after defeating Phil Mickelson in the 1999 US Open at Pinehurst No. 2.

Payne Stewart on the final day. Pinehurst No. 2 has hosted the PGA Championship, Ryder Cup, and US Women's Open. In 2014, it became the first to host men's and women's US Opens in back-to-back weeks. It is also the only course to host all five major USGA events.

HOGAN'S VICTORY

Ben Hogan won the 1940 North and South Open at Pinehurst No. 2. The win helped jump-start his career. Before the event, Hogan hadn't won in seven years. He'd finished second place six times in the prior months. But Hogan won, finishing with a tournament record of 277.

A stone cairn marks the site of the first British Open shot at Prestwick. The original first hole was about 578 yards (529 m).

PRESTWICK

Prestwick is a historic golf course in Scotland. Founded in 1851, it was designed by legendary golfer Old Tom Morris. Morris's layout for the course included 12 holes.

After golfer Allan Robertson's death, Prestwick members organized the first British Open. It was held at Prestwick in 1860. The course hosted the first 12 British Opens with the Royal and Ancient Golf Club of St. Andrews and the Honourable Company of Edinburgh Golfers. It hosted 24 times, with the final time in 1925.

Six of Prestwick's original greens are still used today. The seventeenth hole, Alps, was originally the second hole. Its layout remains unchanged, making it the oldest hole in championship golf. It's named after a large mound that creates a blind second shot into the green. Prestwick also has a stone wall and a railroad line down the right side of the first fairway, along with a bunker interrupting the fairway of the third hole. A cairn marks where the first British Open tee shot was hit.

Prestwick's par-5 Alps hole includes five bunkers, the largest of which is called the Sahara bunker.

ROYAL TROON

Royal Troon is a links-style course in Scotland. Founded in 1878, it hosted its first British Open in 1923 and its tenth British Open in 2024. In 2016, the British Open at Royal Troon featured Phil Mickelson competing against Henrik Stenson. Both players

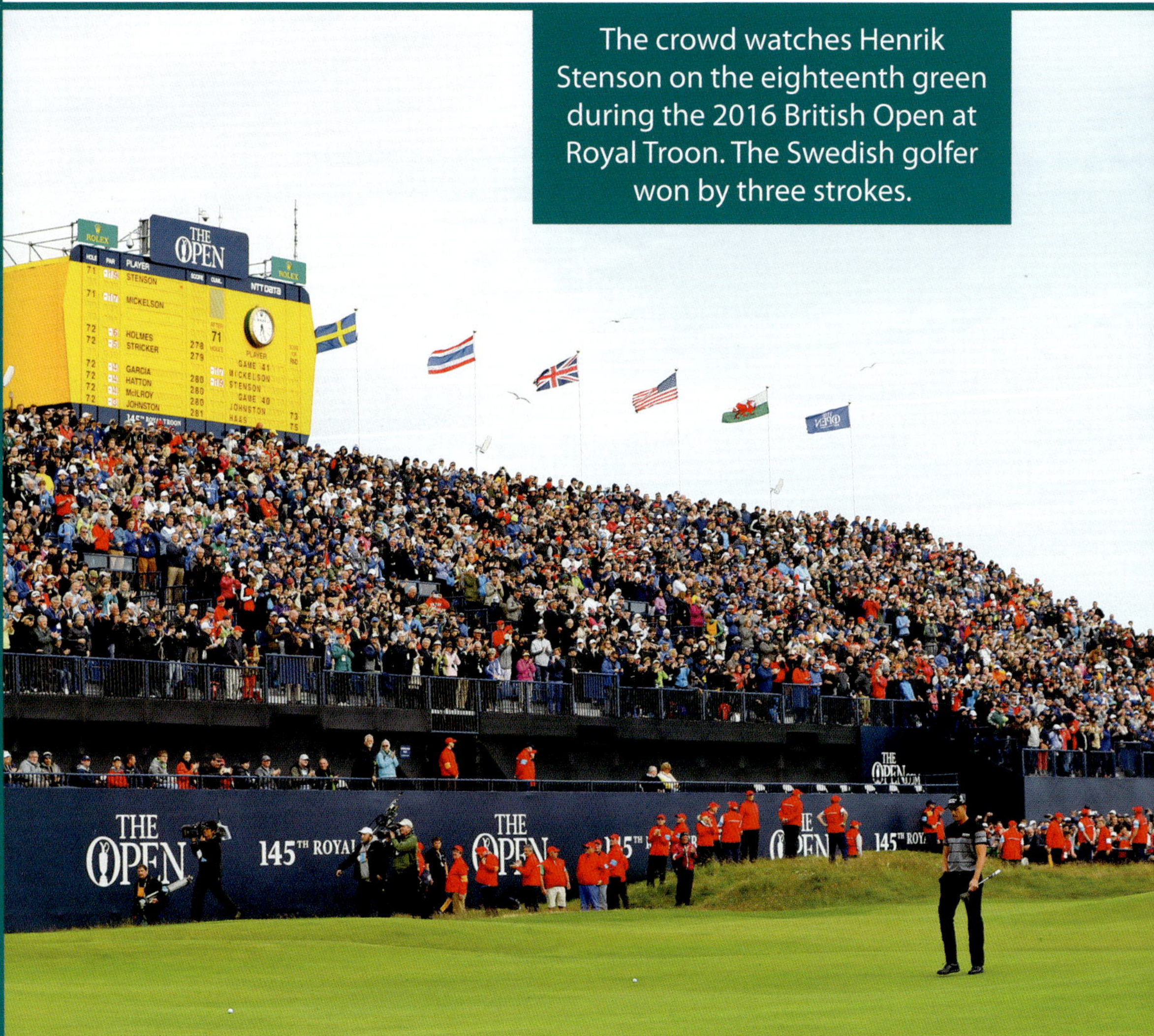

The crowd watches Henrik Stenson on the eighteenth green during the 2016 British Open at Royal Troon. The Swedish golfer won by three strokes.

Royal Troon's Postage Stamp includes five challenging bunkers.

set the course record for 18 holes at 63. Stenson won, breaking a streak of six Americans winning the British Open at Royal Troon.

The course opens along Scotland's west coast for six holes before heading inland. Its eighth hole, the Postage Stamp, is famously tough. The par 3 is the shortest used in the British Open. The challenge lies in the green's size and bunkers. The small green is said to be the size of a postage stamp.

The Postage Stamp has caused many disasters, such as Tiger Woods taking a triple bogey on the hole in 1997. It caused an amateur to take a 15 during the 1950 British Open. But some players, such as Gene Sarazen, have made holes in one.

Brooks Koepka, *right*, celebrates with his caddie, Ricky Elliott, after winning the 2018 US Open at Shinnecock Hills.

SHINNECOCK HILLS

Founded in 1891, New York's Shinnecock Hills is the United States's oldest incorporated golf club. It is also one of the USGA's founding members. The links-style course is the only course to host the US Open in three different centuries. The second US Open was held at Shinnecock Hills in 1896. The tournament wouldn't return to the course for another 90 years. The 1995, 2004, and 2018 US Opens took place at Shinnecock Hills. The course was scheduled to host again in 2026.

For the 2018 US Open, officials expanded the course's length. It changed from 4,423 yards (4,044 m) to 7,445 yards (6,808 m). The course underwent many other changes between 1891 and 1931.

The course's par-3 seventh hole has a Redan green, which is offset from the fairway with a bunker in front. It slopes from the front right to the back left away from the tee. At the 2004 US Open, the heat created a dry surface on the green that was difficult to play on. The USGA had to water it.

Englishman Lee Westwood takes a shot from a bunker on the seventh hole during the 2004 US Open.

ST. ANDREWS OLD COURSE

St. Andrews Old Course is in St. Andrews, Scotland. It is the world's oldest existing golf course. It got its name when the New Course was built next to it in 1895.

The Old Course was built in the 1700s with 22 holes. In 1764, people combined some holes to make them longer. This lowered the course to 18 holes.

Many holes on the Old Course share greens. This is because of how the course was originally played. Golfers played the same holes coming back as they did going out. To relieve congestion, a second hole was cut into the greens. Today, white

St. Andrews Old Course has hosted more British Opens than any other golf course.

Many golfers at the Old Course take photos on Swilcan Bridge, which crosses the stream on the eighteenth hole. Lorena Ochoa posed on the historic bridge after winning the 2007 Women's Open.

flags mark the front nine holes and red flags mark the back nine, except for the eighteenth hole, which has a white flag.

The British Open was first played at the Old Course in 1873. It returned 29 times, including for the 150th British Open in 2022. In 2007, the course hosted its first professional women's tournament.

Tony Finau takes a shot during the 2024 Farmers Insurance Open at Torrey Pines.

TORREY PINES

Torrey Pines is a public golf course in La Jolla, California. It is named after a pine tree that grows wild only in the area. The course is known for its scenic views of the Pacific Ocean and for the challenge it provides for golfers.

There are two courses on the site, the North and the South. Both are used during the Farmers Insurance Open, an annual

PGA Tour tournament. The course is set up with narrow fairways and thick rough, more closely resembling the tough conditions of majors. The South is tougher than the North and has hosted two US Opens.

Torrey Pines first hosted the US Open in 2008, when Tiger Woods had a memorable victory. He was recovering from knee surgery and was visibly in pain during the tournament. Woods fought through the pain to force an 18-hole playoff against Rocco Mediate. Woods won.

Tiger Woods competed in the 2008 US Open at Torrey Pines just two months after having knee surgery.

TPC SAWGRASS

TPC Sawgrass opened in Florida in 1980. It was the first stadium course and Tournament Players Club (TPC) course. Designed by PGA Tour commissioner Deane Beman and Pete and Alice Dye, TPC Sawgrass was built to be the home of the Players Championship.

The course's par-3 seventeenth hole is called Island Green. The original design had a lake partially surrounding the hole.

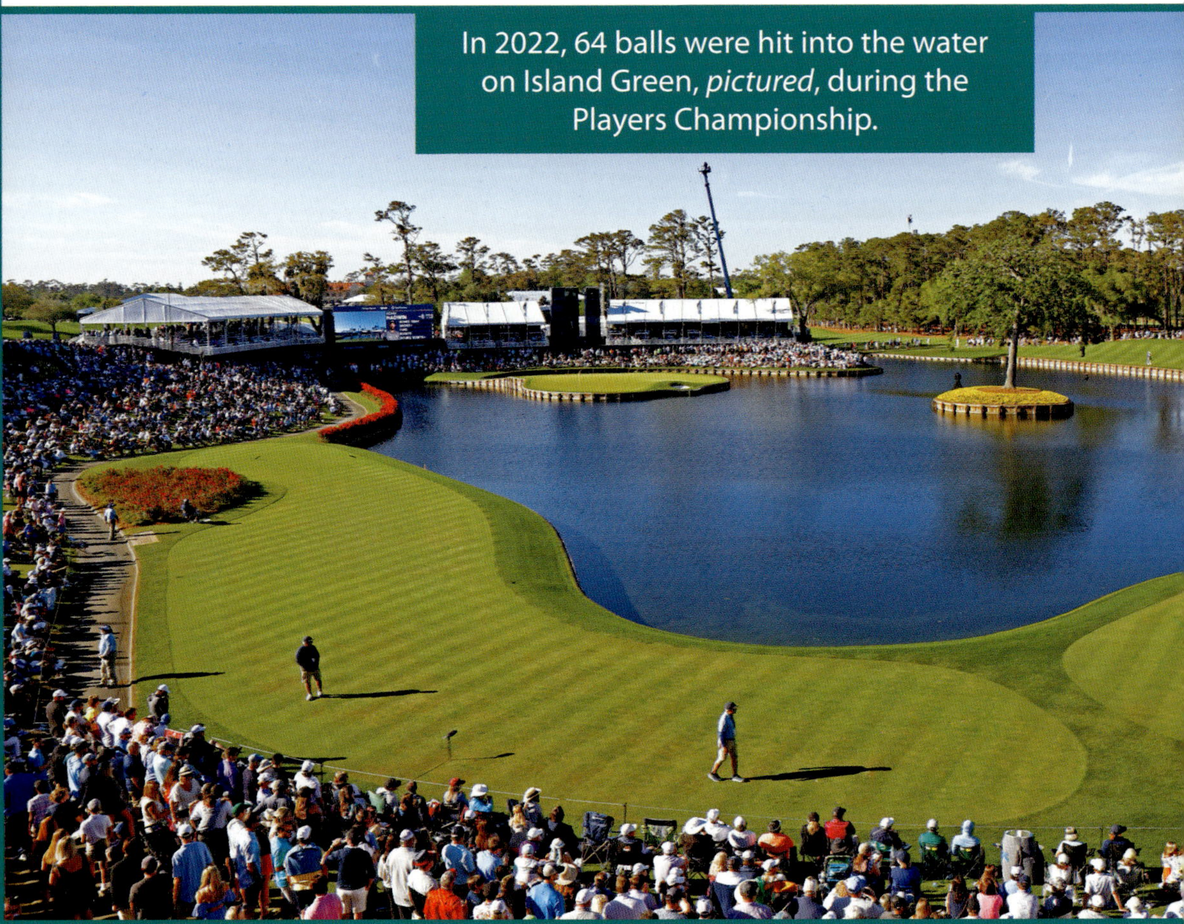

In 2022, 64 balls were hit into the water on Island Green, *pictured*, during the Players Championship.

Jordan Spieth practices on Island Green before competing in the 2016 Players Championship.

But after the ground around the green needed to be dug up, Alice Dye suggested making it an island.

Many fans enjoy watching players at Island Green. There is little room for error, and many shots go into the water. The hole is often a turning point in the Players Championship. It can make or break a player's chances of winning. In 2001, Tiger Woods hit a shot that barely stayed on the green. He was left with a difficult putt. He made it and went on to win his first Players Championship.

TPC SCOTTSDALE

TPC Scottsdale is located near Phoenix, Arizona. It has been home to the annual WM Phoenix Open since 1987. The course has the second-longest streak of hosting a PGA Tour event. The course is used year-round but is known for how it transforms for the WM Phoenix Open.

The course's most famous hole is the sixteenth hole. Tournament organizers put temporary grandstands all the way around the par 3, making it the only fully enclosed hole on the PGA Tour. The grandstand, called the Coliseum, seats more than

Japan's Hideki Matsuyama takes a shot on the Stadium Hole during the 2024 WM Phoenix Open. Golfers competing at this hole often get booed by fans if they make a poor shot.

Desert plants such as cacti appear throughout the TPC Scottsdale course, including on its famous Stadium Hole.

20,000 fans and has nearly 300 skyboxes. In terms of seating capacity, it holds more than the average National Basketball Association arena.

The par-3 sixteenth has been called the loudest hole in golf. Considering that noise is usually frowned upon during play, this makes the hole unique. The hole gives TPC Scottsdale the largest crowds of any golf event.

US team members Mark O'Meara, *left*, and Tiger Woods, *right*, practice during the 1997 Ryder Cup at Valderrama.

VALDERRAMA

Spain's Valderrama course is one of mainland Europe's top courses. It is known for hosting the 1997 Ryder Cup. This marked the first time the Cup was held in continental Europe. The US team started five points behind on the final day, and it came down to the final match between Colin Montgomerie and Scott Hoch. They tied, but the Europeans won 14.5–13.5.

Valderrama's most famous hole is the par-5 seventeenth. It is reachable

in two, but golfers must clear the water in front of the green. Shots that fall short, along with shots that land on the other side of the hazard, go into the water. There have been two double eagles on the hole, both in the Volvo Masters. These were achieved by Miguel Ángel Jiménez in 1994 and Graeme McDowell in 2007. Valderrama has also hosted several European Tour events. In 2023, it began hosting a LIV tournament.

Valderrama's seventeenth hole, *pictured*, was redesigned by Seve Ballesteros for the Ryder Cup. It features a large water hazard.

WINGED FOOT

Winged Foot is in New York. It includes two championship-level courses, the East and the West. Golf architect A. W. Tillinghast designed the course, which opened in 1923. The West course has hosted one PGA Championship and six US Opens, with another scheduled in 2028. The East course has hosted two US Women's Opens and one US Senior Open.

The West Course first hosted the US Open in 1929. Golfer Bobby Jones won the event. In the 2006 US Open, Geoff Ogilvy

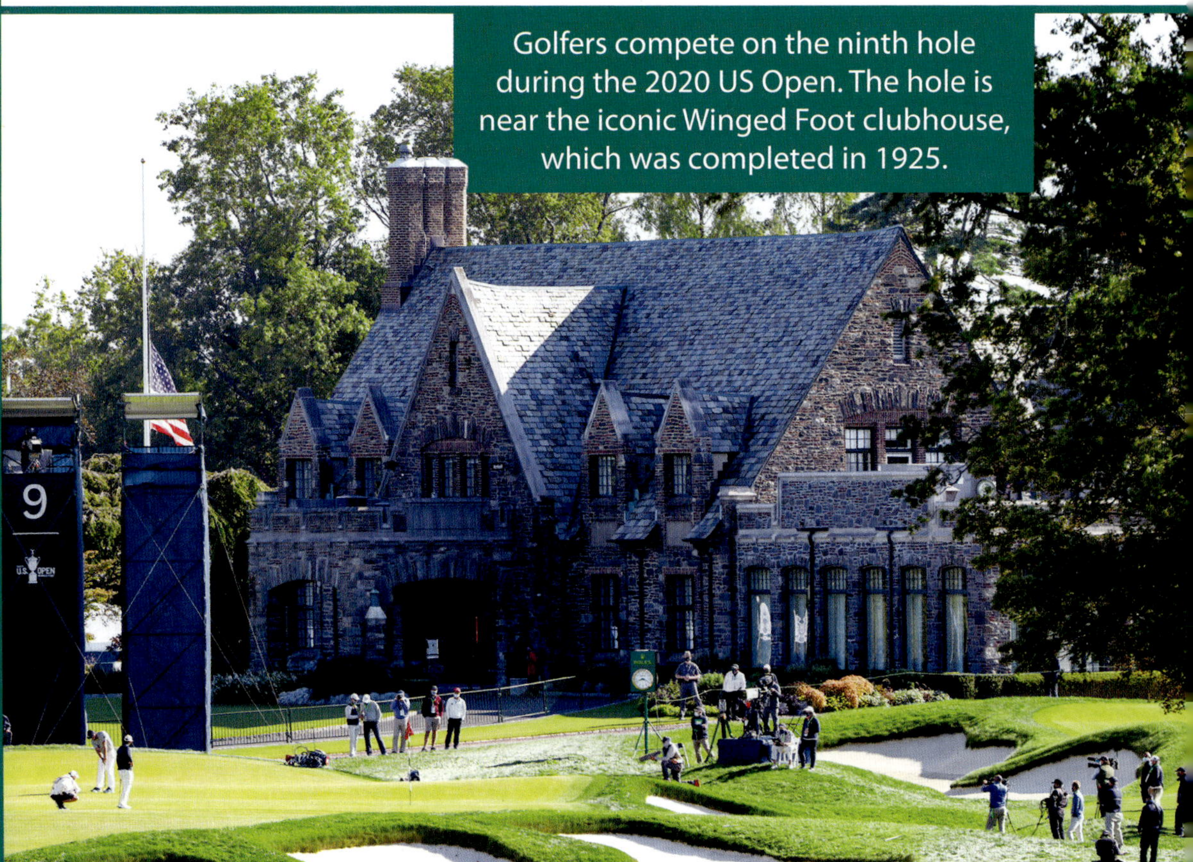

Golfers compete on the ninth hole during the 2020 US Open. The hole is near the iconic Winged Foot clubhouse, which was completed in 1925.

Hale Irwin, *center*, speaks to the crowd after winning the 1974 US Open at Winged Foot.

won without breaking par in any round. The 1974 tournament was called the Massacre at Winged Foot after Hale Irwin won with a score of 7-over. There hasn't been a higher winning score in a major since.

The 2020 US Open at Winged Foot was unique. Due to the COVID-19 pandemic, no spectators were allowed. Only volunteers and neighbors with makeshift grandstands were present.

AMY ALCOTT

Amy Alcott was only 18 years old when she turned pro. In her first season as a pro, she was named Rookie of the Year.

Amy Alcott turned professional in 1975, two years after winning the US Girls' Junior Championship. Five years after turning pro, she won the US Women's Open with a 72-hole scoring record of 280. It was one of five majors Alcott won during her career.

Alcott won 29 times on the LPGA Tour and was inducted into the LPGA and World Golf halls of fame in 1999. In 1988, Alcott started a tradition after winning the Chevron Championship, then titled the Nabisco Dinah Shore. She jumped into the pond by the eighteenth green. She did it again in 1991, and ever since, winners have celebrated in the same way.

Career Earnings: $3,043,307

Major Wins: 5

Tour Wins: 29

Top Ten Finishes in Majors: 30

Solheim Cup Record: N/A

SEVE BALLESTEROS

Spanish golfer Seve Ballesteros turned pro at age 16. Two years later, he finished in second at the 1976 British Open. Ballesteros rocketed to stardom after winning the 1979 British Open. At age 22, he was the event's youngest winner since 1893. He was also the first mainland European winner since 1907.

It was the first of five majors for Ballesteros, who also won 93 tournaments during his career. Some people say he's why the Great Britain–Ireland Ryder Cup team started including continental European golfers. Ballesteros was on the first European team in 1979 and was team captain at Valderrama in 1997. Ballesteros died in 2011.

Seve Ballesteros celebrates after winning the 1979 British Open at Royal Lytham & St. Annes Golf Club. He played the final seven holes in one under par.

Career Earnings: $1,840,357
Major Wins: 5
Tour Wins: 9
Top Ten Finishes in Majors: 20
Ryder Cup Record: 20–12–5

PATTY BERG

Minnesotan Patty Berg has contributed to golf on and off the course. She won three different amateur titles, some more than once, before turning pro in 1940. But a car accident delayed Berg's full-time debut until 1943. She went on to win 60 LPGA Tour events, including the first US Women's Open. It was one of 15 major championships for Berg.

Career Earnings: $190,760
Major Wins: 15
Tour Wins: 60
Top Ten Finishes in Majors: 57
Solheim Cup Record: N/A

Berg was one of the LPGA's 13 founders. She also served as the first president of the LPGA Tour when it was created in 1950. Berg is in several halls of fame, including the World Golf Hall of Fame.

Patty Berg started playing golf when she was 13 years old. Her amateur career started when she won the 1934 Minneapolis City Championship at age 16.

PAT BRADLEY

New Englander Pat Bradley was an amateur before becoming an All-American, one of the top athletes in her sport at Florida International University. She turned pro in 1974, winning her first tournament two years later. Her first major win was the 1980 du Maurier Classic. She also won the 1981 US Women's Open and three majors in 1986. She is one of six women to complete the career grand slam in the four-major era.

Bradley won 31 times on Tour, including nine times after being diagnosed with a thyroid condition in 1988. She was a three-time US Solheim Cup team member, serving as captain in 2000. She is in the World Golf and LPGA halls of fame.

Pat Bradley's first LPGA Tour title was the 1976 Girl Talk Classic.

Career Earnings: $5,291,624
Major Wins: 6
Tour Wins: 31
Top Ten Finishes in Majors: 34
Solheim Cup Record: 2–5–1

JoANNE CARNER

JoAnne Carner won USGA championships at every level. She won the US Girls' Junior Championship in 1956 and the US Women's Amateur five times. In 1971, Carner won her first of two US Women's Opens. Her number of eight USGA wins is the most among female golfers. Carner also won 43 LPGA Tour events.

JoAnne Carner smiles with the Cox Trophy after winning her fifth US Women's Amateur title. She is the only woman to have won the US Women's Amateur, US Girls' Junior Championship, and US Open.

Carner captained the US Solheim Cup team in 1994. At age 64, she played in the Chevron Championship, becoming the oldest player in LPGA history to make the cut. Carner also played in the 2021 US Senior Women's Open at age 82, setting another record for oldest player in a USGA championship. Carner is in the World Golf and LPGA halls of fame.

Career Earnings: $2,306,582

Major Wins: 2

Tour Wins: 43

Top Ten Finishes in Majors: 32

Solheim Cup Record: 1–0–0 (nonplaying captain)

BILLY CASPER

Billy Casper won 33 PGA Tour events during the 1960s. He won 51 total titles. At the time of Casper's death in 2015, he had the seventh-most wins in PGA Tour history. However, Casper was often overshadowed by the "Big Three" golfers of his era.

Career Earnings: $1,691,583
Major Wins: 3
Tour Wins: 51
Top Ten Finishes in Majors: 24
Ryder Cup Record: 20–10–7

Casper defeated Arnold Palmer in the 1966 US Open. Casper overcame a seven-stroke deficit on the back nine to tie with Palmer. He then defeated Palmer in a playoff. It was one of three major wins for Casper. He also won the 1959 US Open and 1970 Masters. He was an eight-time US Ryder Cup team member, serving as captain in 1969. Casper holds the US record for most Ryder Cup points.

Billy Casper takes a shot in the 1968 British Open at Carnoustie Golf Links.

Ben Crenshaw, *center*, competes at Augusta National during the 1976 Masters.

BEN CRENSHAW

Texan Ben Crenshaw won his first golf tournament in fourth grade. He continued playing in college, winning three national championships at the University of Texas. In 1973, Crenshaw won his final college championship and first PGA Tour. He wouldn't win again until 1976, when he had three victories. Crenshaw won 19 PGA Tour events during his career, including two Masters. His final PGA Tour victory was the 1995 Masters.

Crenshaw was a four-time US Ryder Cup team member, serving as captain in 1999. Crenshaw was easygoing and known as "Gentle Ben." He later worked as a course architect. In 2002, Crenshaw was inducted into the World Golf Hall of Fame.

Career Earnings: $10,250,240

Major Wins: 2

Tour Wins: 19

Top Ten Finishes in Majors: 27

Ryder Cup Record: 3–8–1

Crenshaw takes a shot during the 1995 Ryder Cup at Oak Hill Country Club.

LAURA DAVIES

Laura Davies turned pro in 1985. The England native won the Belgium Open in her first year on the LET. The following year, she won the 1986 Women's Open.

In 1987, Davies become the first English player to win the US Women's Open. It was her first major, since the Women's Open wasn't yet a major. Davies later won the 1994 and 1996 LPGA Championships and the 1996 du Maurier Classic.

Laura Davies holds the Women's Open trophy, *left*, and the US Women's Open trophy, *right*, in 1987. That year, she won the US Women's Open by two strokes.

In 2023, Laura Davies competed in the Women's PGA Championship. As of 2023, she has played in 133 majors.

Davies played in 12 consecutive Solheim Cups. On the Women's Senior Tour, Davies won the US Senior Women's Open and the LPGA Senior Championship. Between the LET and LPGA, Davies won 65 tournaments. She was named an LPGA Top-50 player in 2000 and is in the World Golf Hall of Fame. In 2014, England's Queen Elizabeth II gave Davies the title of dame for her accomplishments.

Career Earnings: $9,255,441

Major Wins: 4

Tour Wins: 20

Top Ten Finishes in Majors: 22

Solheim Cup Record: 22–18–6

Babe Didrikson Zaharias was known for her competitive spirit and long-distance golf drives. She holds the LPGA record for being the fastest to reach 10 wins, 20 wins, and 30 wins.

BABE DIDRIKSON ZAHARIAS

Babe Didrikson Zaharias was one of the greatest female athletes of the twentieth century. The Texan won two gold medals in track and field at the 1932 Olympic Games. She played basketball and baseball before taking up golf. Fans flocked to watch Didrikson Zaharias's athleticism and showmanship.

Didrikson Zaharias earned 41 professional victories and ten majors. At one point, she won 17 consecutive tournaments. Her first of three US Women's Open titles came in 1948. In 1954, she won the US Women's Open after having cancer surgery the previous year. She died two years later at age 45.

Career Earnings:	$66,237
Major Wins:	10
Tour Wins:	41
Top Ten Finishes in Majors:	N/A
Solheim Cup Record:	N/A

Didrikson Zaharias was cofounder of the LPGA. In 1945, she also became the only woman to make a tournament cut in a men's PGA Tour event. She won many awards, including the 1950 Associated Press Woman Athlete of the Half-Century. Didrikson Zaharias is in the LPGA and World Golf halls of fame.

Babe Didrikson Zaharias smiles after winning the 1954 US Women's Open at Salem Country Club in Massachusetts. She won the tournament by 12 strokes.

ERNIE ELS

South African Ernie Els made a name for himself on his first PGA Tour year. His first Tour win came at the 1994 US Open, and he was named Rookie of the Year. Between 1991 and 1992, Els won on South Africa's golf tour seven times. In 1993, he became the first man to shoot in the 60s in each of the British Open's four rounds. He holds the record for most all-time

Ernie Els hits a shot during a playoff round at the 1994 US Open. He defeated Loren Roberts and Colin Montgomerie to claim the title.

In 2023, Ernie Els competed in the Principal Charity Classic, a PGA Tour Champions event.

British Open rounds in the 60s, with 42. Els won the US Open and British Open twice.

Between the PGA Tour, PGA Tour Champions, and international tours, Els has won more than 75 times.

Career Earnings: $49,385,600
Major Wins: 4
Tour Wins: 19
Top Ten Finishes in Majors: 35
Ryder Cup Record: N/A

Between 1994 and 2009, Els was inside the Official World Golf Ranking's Top 10 for a record 758 weeks. Due to his effortless swing, Els was nicknamed "the Big Easy." In 2011, he was inducted into the World Golf Hall of Fame.

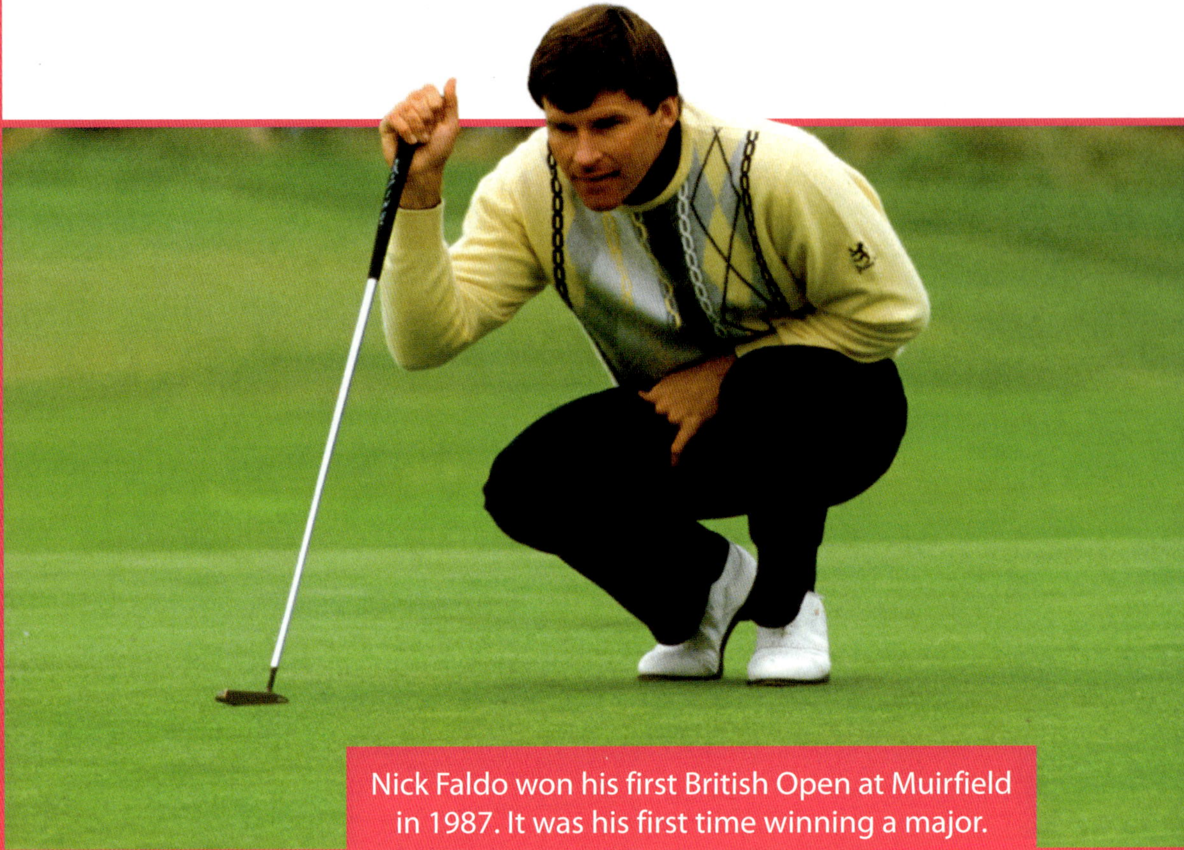

Nick Faldo won his first British Open at Muirfield in 1987. It was his first time winning a major.

NICK FALDO

Many golf fans know Nick Faldo through his TV commentary. His golf career was also notable. Faldo started playing golf at age 14 after watching Jack Nicklaus in the 1971 Masters. Six years later, Faldo became the youngest player to qualify for the Ryder Cup.

Faldo earned more than 40 professional wins, including six majors, and spent 98 weeks as the world's number-one golfer. He also held the record for most Ryder Cup career points. Faldo split his six majors evenly between the British Open and the Masters. In his third British Open, Faldo became the first British player to win three times since the 1930s and 1940s.

After retiring, Faldo began covering golf tournaments on TV. He became the lead analyst for CBS and the Golf Channel. He also worked with the BBC. In 2009, Queen Elizabeth II knighted Faldo.

Career Earnings: $6,045,627
Major Wins: 6
Tour Wins: 9
Top Ten Finishes in Majors: 26
Ryder Cup Record: 23–19–4

Nick Faldo, *left*, appeared with Golf Channel sports commentator Terry Gannon, *right*, during the 2011 Players Championship.

RAYMOND FLOYD

Career Earnings: $18,948,018
Major Wins: 4
Tour Wins: 22
Top Ten Finishes in Majors: 28
Ryder Cup Record: 12–16–3

Raymond Floyd won 22 PGA tournaments and four majors. In 1992, he won his final PGA Tour event at age 49. Later that year, he won the PGA Tour Champions. It was the first time a player won both events in the same year.

Floyd almost won a major in four different decades. He won the 1969 PGA Championship, the 1976 Masters, the 1982 PGA Championship, and the 1986 US Open. He almost won the 1990 Masters but lost in a playoff. Floyd also played on eight Ryder Cup teams, serving as captain in 1989. That same year, he was inducted into the World Golf Hall of Fame.

Masters winner Raymond Floyd, *right*, smiles as Jack Nicklaus helps him put on his green Jacket in 1976.

WALTER HAGEN

Walter Hagen was a major golf star during the sport's early years. His showmanship and skills attracted crowds. The New Yorker won his first US Open in 1914, setting a course record with a first round of 68. Hagen won again in 1919.

In the 1920s, Hagen won four British Opens and five PGA Championships. He was the first American-born golfer to win the Claret Jug. He won four of his five PGA Championships in consecutive years. He also served as US team captain for the first six Ryder Cups. Hagen died at age 76 in 1969. In 1974, he was in the first class of players elected to the World Golf Hall of Fame.

Walter Hagen is considered one of the first professional golfers. He is often referred to as the "Father of Professional Golf."

Career Earnings: $15,675

Major Wins: 11

Tour Wins: 45

Top Ten Finishes in Majors: 33

Ryder Cup Record: 7–1–1

PADRAIG HARRINGTON

Padraig Harrington holds the Claret Jug after winning the 2007 British Open. He defeated Sergio Garcia in a playoff to win the title.

Irishman Padraig Harrington won his first professional tournament, the 1996 Spanish Open, after just ten events on the European tour. Three years later, he qualified for the European Ryder Cup team. Harrington was a Ryder Cup player, vice-captain, or captain for the next 20 years.

In 2006, Harrington was ranked Europe's number-one golfer. The next year, he became the first Irishman to win the Irish Open in 25 years. He also became the first Irishman to win the British Open in 60 years. He won again in 2008, becoming the first European in 102 years to win in back-to-back years. Harrington's success continued with a PGA Championship that year. He has received many awards, including the European, PGA Tour, and PGA of America Player of the Year awards.

Career Earnings: $26,172,322
Major Wins: 3
Tour Wins: 6
Top Ten Finishes in Majors: 16
Ryder Cup Record: 9–13–3

SANDRA HAYNIE

Career Earnings: $556,477

Major Wins: 4

Tour Wins: 42

Top Ten Finishes in Majors: 25

Solheim Cup Record: N/A

Texan Sandra Haynie was a frequent LPGA Tour winner. She won her first title, the 1962 Austin Civitan Open, at age 19. It was her second year on tour. It was the first of Haynie's 42 Tour victories.

Haynie's first major win was the Women's PGA Championship. Almost a decade later, she won the 1974 Women's PGA Championship and the US Women's Open. At the time, she was the second person to win both events in the same year. Eight years later, she won her fourth major, the 1982 CP Women's Open. Haynie spent 12 years inside the Top 10 on the LPGA Tour Money List. In 1977, she was inducted into the LPGA and World Golf halls of fame.

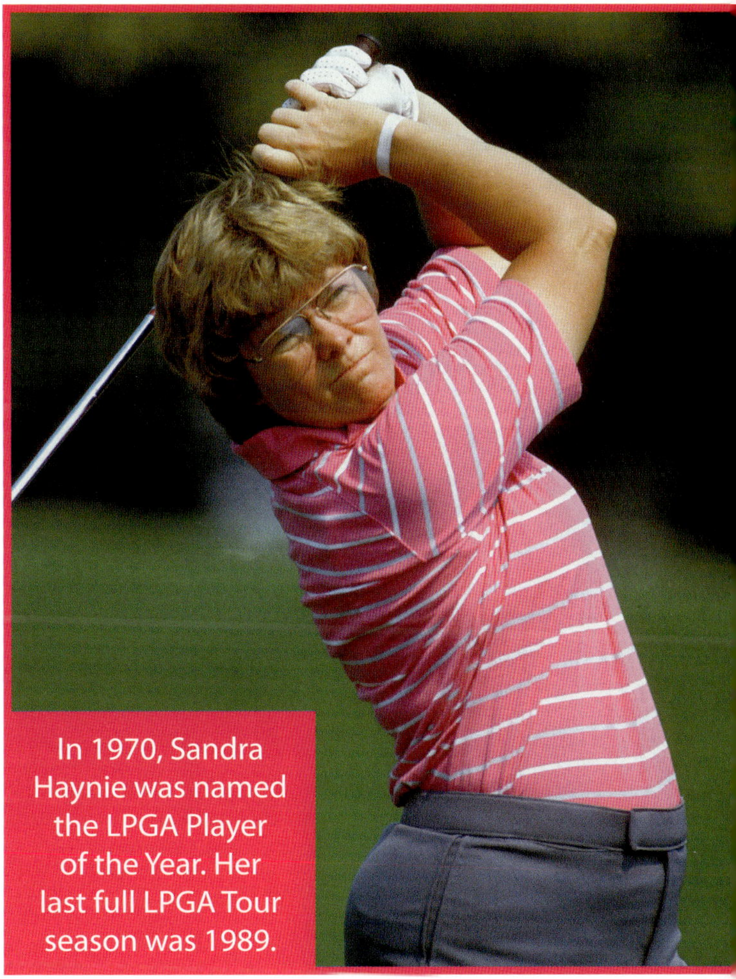

In 1970, Sandra Haynie was named the LPGA Player of the Year. Her last full LPGA Tour season was 1989.

BEN HOGAN

Ben Hogan joined the PGA Tour in 1931. His only victory during the decade was the 1938 Hershey Four-Ball. In 1940, the Texan finally won the North & South Open.

Hogan won 52 PGA Tour events in the 1940s, including 13 events in 1946. One was his first major, the PGA Championship. But in 1949, Hogan was injured in a car crash. Doctors doubted he would golf again.

Ben Hogan hits a shot during the 1947 Los Angeles Open at Riviera Country Club. He went on to win the event. He also won it in 1942 and 1948.

Ben Hogan, *second from left*, accepts the 1950 US Open trophy with his wife, Valerie, *left*. It was Hogan's second time winning the event.

Hogan returned at the 1950 US Open. On the final day, he was in contention to win. Entering the eighteenth hole, he needed a par to force a playoff. After a drive down the middle, Hogan hit a 1 iron onto the green. He parred the hole and won the playoff.

Career Earnings: $332,516
Major Wins: 9
Tour Wins: 64
Top Ten Finishes in Majors: 40
Ryder Cup Record: 3–0–0

Three years later, Hogan won the Masters with a tournament record of 274. He then won the US Open and British Open. Hogan became the first to win those three tournaments in the same year. Hogan won 64 total times, and nine of those wins were majors. He was a four-time Ryder Cup team member and three-time captain.

JULI INKSTER

From 1980 to 1982, Juli Inkster won three straight US Women's Amateur titles. She was the first person to do so since 1934. Inkster went on to win two majors in her first full year on the LPGA Tour in 1984. She won her final major in 2002 at age 42, becoming the second-oldest US Women's Open winner.

Inkster won each of the four majors in her career. She is one of six women to achieve a career grand slam in the LPGA's four-major era. She won 31 times on Tour. Inkster was also a nine-time US Solheim Cup team member and three-time captain. She is in the LPGA and World Golf halls of fame.

In 1984, Juli Inkster won the Chevron Championship and the du Maurier Classic. She was also named Rookie of the Year.

Career Earnings: $14,018,391
Major Wins: 7
Tour Wins: 31
Top Ten Finishes in Majors: 30
Solheim Cup Record: 15–12–7

HALE IRWIN

Hale Irwin played golf and football at the University of Colorado. As a defensive back, he was an All-Conference honoree. As a golfer, he was a college champion, winning the title in 1967. Irwin turned pro in 1968 and went on to win the US Open three times. His final US Open victory came at age 45, making him the oldest player to ever win the tournament.

Irwin was a five-time member of the US Ryder Cup team. He also won two US Senior Opens. He had 45 tournament wins on the PGA Tour Champions, which was a record number until 2023. Irwin was inducted into the World Golf Hall of Fame in 1992.

Hale Irwin competes during the 1979 US Open, which he won. He won the tournament again in 1990.

Career Earnings: $54,317,030

Major Wins: 3

Tour Wins: 20

Top Ten Finishes in Majors: 20

Ryder Cup Record: 13–5–2

BOBBY JONES

Golf icon Bobby Jones was so popular that even his putter, called Calamity Jane, was famous. He achieved success without ever turning pro. Between 1923 and 1930, Jones won 13 events, seven of which were majors.

In 1930, Jones became the only player to win a grand slam in a single year. At the time, the four majors were the British Amateur, British Open, US Open, and US Amateur. Jones won them all that year before retiring at age 28. He won the US Amateur five times, the US Open four times, the British Open three times, and the British Amateur once.

Bobby Jones grew up near East Lake Country Club in Atlanta, Georgia. He won his first golf tournament there at age six.

Career Earnings: N/A
Major Wins: 13
Tour Wins: 34
Top Ten Finishes in Majors: 27
Ryder Cup Record: N/A

Bobby Jones won the British Open in 1926, 1927, and 1930. He was the only amateur player to win the tournament three times.

Jones cofounded Augusta National Golf Club and the Masters. It was the only tournament Jones played in after retiring. Jones died in 1971 at age 69. The USGA's highest honor is the Bob Jones Award, presented annually since 1955.

BROOKS KOEPKA

Career Earnings: $77,611,865
Major Wins: 5
Tour Wins: 9
Top Ten Finishes in Majors: 18
Ryder Cup Record: 4–3–1

Through 2023, Brooks Koepka has won nine tournaments, five of which were majors. His first major win was the 2017 US Open. Koepka won the tournament again in 2018. He also won back-to-back PGA Championships in 2018 and 2019. It was the first time a golfer had won consecutive titles in two majors simultaneously. Koepka won the PGA Championship for a third time in 2023.

Starting in 2018, Koepka spent 47 weeks ranked as the world's number-one golfer. In 2022, he joined the LIV Tour, serving as captain of the Smash GC team. He won one event in each of his first two years with LIV.

Brooks Koepka holds the Wanamaker Trophy after winning the 2023 PGA Championship. The victory made him the twentieth player to win five majors.

NELLY KORDA

Career Earnings: $11,944,144
Major Wins: 2
Tour Wins: 14
Top Ten Finishes in Majors: 11
Solheim Cup Record: 7–4–1

Floridian Nelly Korda started playing golf at a young age. In 2016, the 18-year-old turned pro. That year, she earned her LPGA Tour card for 2017. Throughout the late 2010s and into the 2020s, Korda rocketed to stardom. In 2021, she nabbed four victories. One was Korda's first major, the Women's PGA Championship. Later that year, Korda earned her first gold medal at the 2020 Olympics in Tokyo, Japan. This event was postponed to 2021 due to the COVID-19 pandemic. She won the women's individual golf event with a score of 17 under par. By November 2021, Korda was number one in the Women's World Golf Rankings.

Nelly Korda competes in the first round of the 2024 Women's PGA Championship. The event took place at Sahalee Country Club in Washington State.

As of 2024, Korda has won 14 times on the LPGA Tour. One of those wins was Korda's second major, the 2024 Chevron Championship. The victory marked Korda's fifth consecutive tournament win that year. This winning streak has only been accomplished by others twice in men's golf and twice in women's golf. As of July 2024, Korda held the number-one spot in the Women's World Golf Rankings and was set to compete in the 2024 Olympics in Paris, France.

BERNHARD LANGER

German Bernhard Langer won the Masters twice, in 1985 and 1993, and was the first to be ranked number one when the Official World Golf Ranking began in 1986. Most of Langer's early victories came on the European Tour, where he won 42 times. Langer was also a ten-time Ryder Cup European team member, serving as captain in 2004.

Bernhard Langer wears a green jacket after winning his second Masters in 1993. He won the tournament by four strokes.

In 2023, 65-year-old Bernhard Langer won the US Senior Open. It was his second time winning the event.

Langer joined the PGA Tour Champions at age 50. He won at least one tournament in each of his first 17 years. With 46 wins, he holds the record for most wins by any PGA Tour Champions member. The same record applies to Langer's 12 major wins. He is the only player to win all five PGA Tour Champions majors. In 2024, Langer planned to make his forty-first and final appearance at the Masters. However, he suffered an injury and couldn't play.

Career Earnings: $67,898,139
Major Wins: 2
Tour Wins: 3
Top Ten Finishes in Majors: 19
Ryder Cup Record: 21–15–6

NANCY LOPEZ

In the 1980s, Nancy Lopez helped women's golf grow with her charismatic personality and success. She almost broke through as an amateur in 1975. She had just graduated from high school when she finished second in the US Women's Open. Lopez finished in second place in the event three more times.

Nancy Lopez takes a shot during the 1978 Women's PGA Championship. She won the event, claiming her first major title.

Lopez is on the short list of three-time Women's PGA Championship winners. She won 48 total tournaments, including nine wins in her rookie year of 1978. Lopez also played on the 1990 US Solheim Cup team and served as captain in 2005. In 1987, she was inducted into the World Golf and LPGA halls of fame. The LPGA named the Nancy Lopez Golf Achievement Award after her.

Career Earnings: $4,897,457
Major Wins: 3
Tour Wins: 48
Top Ten Finishes in Majors: 26
Solheim Cup Record: 2–1–0

RORY McILROY

Career Earnings: $80,893,763
Major Wins: 4
Tour Wins: 26
Top Ten Finishes in Majors: 30
Ryder Cup Record: 16–13–1

At age nine, Irishman Rory McIlroy won the 1998 Doral Junior Under-10 World Championship. As an amateur, McIlroy won titles in Ireland and across Europe. He received a silver medal for being the lowest-scoring amateur at the 2007 British Open. That year, McIlroy became the youngest golfer to earn a European Tour card.

McIlroy's first PGA win came in 2010, followed by a victory at the 2011 US Open. His 16-under total was the lowest total score in tournament history. He won again in 2012 and twice in 2014. McIlroy was the third golfer to win four majors by age 25. Since 2010, McIlroy has frequently participated in the Ryder Cup.

Rory McIlroy competes in the 2014 Deutsche Bank Championship at TPC Boston in Massachusetts.

PHIL MICKELSON

Californian Phil Mickelson started as an amateur. From 1986 to 1988, he was named national Junior Player of the Year three straight times. He went on to win three college championships as part of the Arizona State team. In 1991, Mickelson won his first PGA Tour event as an amateur, becoming the fourth to do so at that stage.

Phil Mickelson jumps into the air after winning the 2004 Masters. During the tournament's final round, Mickelson had birdies on two of the last three holes.

Phil Mickelson's nickname is Lefty because he swings from the left side. However, he is not left-handed. He learned to swing by mirroring his father, who was right-handed.

After turning pro, Mickelson became one of the world's best players. His outgoing personality attracted fans, and he had a popular rivalry with Tiger Woods. But Mickelson still hadn't won a major.

After 42 appearances, Mickelson finally won the 2004 Masters. He won five more majors, including the 2021 PGA Championship. At age 50, Mickelson became the oldest player to win a major.

Mickelson holds the record for the most times representing the United States in the Ryder Cup, having done so 12 times as of 2023. He was in every Ryder Cup from 1995 to 2018. In June 2022, Mickelson joined LIV Golf.

Career Earnings: $96,572,310
Major Wins: 6
Tour Wins: 45
Top Ten Finishes in Majors: 40
Ryder Cup Record: 18–22–7

JOHNNY MILLER

During his career, Johnny Miller had 25 PGA Tour wins, including two majors. His most famous victory was the 1973 US Open. Before that, Miller had won only two tournaments in more than three years on the Tour. Miller entered the final round six strokes behind.

Miller heard a voice in his head tell him to open his stance, and the suggestion proved correct. Miller shot an eight-under 63, a record for the tournament's final round. It was enough for a comeback win.

Miller won eight tournaments in 1974, four in 1975, and three in 1976. He capped off 1976 by winning the British Open. Miller achieved 15 wins over the three-year span.

Johnny Miller holds the US Open trophy after winning the 1973 tournament at Oakmont Country Club. Many fans consider his final round in the event one of the greatest rounds in golf history.

Miller later became a TV golf commentator. He was known for his blunt and colorful descriptions. Miller retired from broadcasting in 2019.

Career Earnings: $2,747,484
Major Wins: 2
Tour Wins: 25
Top Ten Finishes in Majors: 17
Ryder Cup Record: 2–2–2

Johnny Miller, *center*, competes in the 1975 Masters. He came in second place that year.

BYRON NELSON

Byron Nelson turned pro in 1932. Over the next 14 years, he dominated the sport with 52 titles. His first major win was the 1937 Masters, which earned him the nickname "Lord Byron." Nelson also figured out how to use steel-shaft golf clubs effectively, giving him a powerful swing. Nelson won the Masters again in 1942.

Byron Nelson was born near Waxahachie, Texas. In 1968, the Texas Victory Open tournament changed its name to the Byron Nelson Classic in his honor.

Byron Nelson signs autographs during the 1943 All-American Open, also known as the Tam O'Shanter Open. Nelson won the event four times, in 1941, 1942, 1944, and 1945.

Nelson won the 1939 US Open and the 1940 and 1945 PGA Championships. His 1945 victory was part of a winning streak. He won 18 tournaments, with a record 11 consecutive tournaments. From 1944 to 1946, Nelson won 34 tournaments. After 1946, he retired.

After retiring, Nelson taught several players, including Tom Watson. He worked in television and was a nonplaying captain for the 1965 Ryder Cup team. Nelson is in the World Golf Hall of Fame. A Texas golf tournament is named after him.

Career Earnings: $190,256

Major Wins: 5

Tour Wins: 52

Top Ten Finishes in Majors: 28

Ryder Cup Record: 3–1–0

JACK NICKLAUS

After entering the golf world, Jack Nicklaus quickly became a household name. The popular golfer was nicknamed "The Golden Bear." He was one of the "Big Three" golfers of the 1960s.

He won the 1986 Masters, earning his sixth green jacket, the most won by any player. At age 46, Nicklaus was also the oldest champion in Masters history. His six Masters titles are part of 18 majors he won during his career, the most won by any golfer. Nicklaus's first PGA Tour victory was the 1962 US Open. He won three British Opens, four US Opens, and five PGA Championships.

Nicklaus finished his career with 93 wins, 73 of which

Career Earnings: $9,106,238

Major Wins: 18

Tour Wins: 73

Top Ten Finishes in Majors: 73

Ryder Cup Record: 17–8–3

Jack Nicklaus poses with the trophy after winning his third US Open at Pebble Beach in 1972.

were on the PGA Tour. He retired with the second-most PGA Tour wins. Nicklaus later worked as a course designer. He is also the founder and host of the Memorial Tournament.

Jack Nicklaus watches his putt on the seventeenth hole during the final round of the 1986 Masters. He got a birdie on the hole, putting him in the lead.

GREG NORMAN

Australian Greg Norman has had 91 professional victories. He held the number-one spot in the World Golf Rankings for 331 weeks, a record until 2004. He also won the British Open twice.

But Norman's losses are also part of his legacy. He finished in second place eight times at majors. At the 1996 Masters, Norman had a six-stroke lead in the final round but lost by five strokes.

Greg Norman won the British Open in 1986 and 1993.

Norman's nickname is the "Great White Shark," and many companies use his shark logo. One is a golf clothing brand. Norman is also the founding CEO of LIV Golf. He was elected to the World Golf Hall of Fame in 2001.

Career Earnings: $15,182,769

Major Wins: 2

Tour Wins: 20

Top Ten Finishes in Majors: 30

Ryder Cup Record: N/A

LORENA OCHOA

After a successful amateur career in her home country of Mexico, Lorena Ochoa came to the United States to attend the University of Arizona. There, she won NCAA Player of the Year honors twice. In 2003, she also won the Nancy Lopez Award. Ochoa joined the LPGA's developmental tour after her sophomore year.

Ochoa moved up to the LPGA in 2003 and was named Rookie of the Year after eight top-ten finishes. Ochoa went on to win 21 times from 2006 to 2008. During that span, she won two majors. From 2007 to 2010, Ochoa was the world's number-one golfer for a record 158 consecutive weeks. She is in the LPGA and World Golf halls of fame.

Career Earnings: $14,863,331
Major Wins: 2
Tour Wins: 27
Top Ten Finishes in Majors: 18
Solheim Cup Record: N/A

Lorena Ochoa hits a shot during the 2008 Chevron Championship at Mission Hills Country Club. She won the tournament by five strokes.

SE RI PAK

South Korean Se Ri Pak gained fame after winning the 1998 US Women's Open. At age 20, she was the tournament's youngest winner. She had won the Women's

Se Ri Pak holds the trophy after winning the 1998 Women's PGA Championship. Before this victory, she won 30 tournaments as an amateur in South Korea.

Se Ri Pak takes a shot during the 1998 US Women's Open at Blackwolf Run resort in Wisconsin. Pak defeated amateur Jenny Chuasiriporn to claim the title.

PGA Championship a few weeks prior, and her success helped start a golf revolution in South Korea. Pak became known for one of her shots during the 1998 Open. During the playoff, she took off her shoes and socks to stand in the water and hit a shot out of the rough.

Pak is on the short list of three-time Women's PGA Championship winners. She finished her career with five major victories and 25 LPGA Tour wins. She is in the LPGA and World Golf halls of fame.

Career Earnings: $12,583,712

Major Wins: 5

Tour Wins: 25

Top Ten Finishes in Majors: 22

Solheim Cup Record: N/A

ARNOLD PALMER

Arnold Palmer celebrates after winning the 1960 US Open at Colorado's Cherry Hills Country Club. Palmer came back from seven strokes behind to win the title.

Arnold Palmer boosted golf's popularity in the late 1950s and early 1960s. His bold play and charming personality attracted many fans, who nicknamed him "the King" and called themselves Arnie's Army. Palmer was one of the era's "Big Three" golfers. He won 29 times between 1960 and 1963. Palmer won the Masters and the British Open twice in that span.

Palmer also helped boost American interest in the British Open. Before he played in the event in 1960, few US players had participated since World War II. Palmer's 1961 and 1962 British Open victories made the tournament more popular with Americans.

The one major Palmer never won was the PGA Championship. He was the runner-up three times and played in the event a record 37 times. Palmer was the first four-time Masters winner. He held the record for most Ryder Cup career points until 1997. He also popularized mixing lemonade and iced tea, a drink known as an Arnold Palmer.

Career Earnings: $1,904,668
Major Wins: 7
Tour Wins: 62
Top Ten Finishes in Majors: 38
Ryder Cup Record: 22–8–2

Fans watch Arnold Palmer compete in the 1962 British Open at Royal Troon. He won the event with a score of 276.

INBEE PARK

Career Earnings: $18,262,344
Major Wins: 7
Tour Wins: 21
Top Ten Finishes in Majors: 35
Solheim Cup Record: N/A

Inbee Park's first LPGA Tour win in 2008 was record breaking. At age 19, the South Korean became the youngest player to win the US Women's Open. Four years later, she won the 2012 Evian Masters. The tournament wasn't a major at the time, but Park has since been given credit for completing a Super Career Grand Slam.

In 2013, Park won the season's first three majors, becoming the first to do so since Babe Didrikson Zaharias. She won the Women's PGA Championship every year from 2013 to 2015. Park became the second player to win three consecutive times. Through the 2023 season, Park won seven majors. In 2016, she became the youngest player to qualify for the LPGA Hall of Fame.

Inbee Park competes during the Honda LPGA Thailand tournament in 2014. She came in second place.

Gary Player celebrates after making a birdie during the 1961 Masters. He went on to win the tournament by one stroke.

GARY PLAYER

Career Earnings: $12,098,058
Major Wins: 9
Tour Wins: 24
Top Ten Finishes in Majors: 44
Ryder Cup Record: N/A

Gary Player was one of the "Big Three" of the 1960s. The South African's first Masters victory came in 1961, when he defeated Arnold Palmer to become the tournament's first international winner. Player went on to compete in a record 52 straight Masters.

Player also played in 46 consecutive British Opens. He won three, each in a different decade. His first victory came in 1959, followed by wins in 1968 and 1974. Player won three Senior British Opens in his career too. Overall, he won nine majors in his PGA career, the fourth most of any player in history.

BETSY RAWLS

Career Earnings: $302,664
Major Wins: 8
Tour Wins: 55
Top Ten Finishes in Majors: N/A
Solheim Cup Record: N/A

Betsy Rawls started playing golf at age 17. Four years later, she won the first of back-to-back Texas Amateur tournaments. Rawls finished second in the 1950 US Women's Open. She joined the LPGA Tour in 1951, winning the US Women's Open that year. During the next 12 years, Rawls won at least two events per season.

In 1959, Rawls won ten events, setting a record for most money earned in a season. This record lasted four years. Rawls was the first four-time US Women's Open winner. In total, she won eight majors and 55 LPGA events. Rawls also served as LPGA president and tournament director. She is in the LPGA and World Golf halls of fame.

Betsy Rawls's eight major wins include the 1953, 1957, and 1960 US Women's Opens. She also won the 1959 and 1969 Women's PGA Championships.

GENE SARAZEN

Gene Sarazen was a star golfer in the 1920s and 1930s. He was the first to achieve a career grand slam. He won the US Open twice, the PGA Championship three times, and the British Open and Masters once.

Sarazen's Masters victory was due to one of the most famous shots in golf history. His second shot on the par-5 fifteenth hole went in from 220 yards (201 m) out for a double eagle. People called it the "Shot Heard 'Round the World."

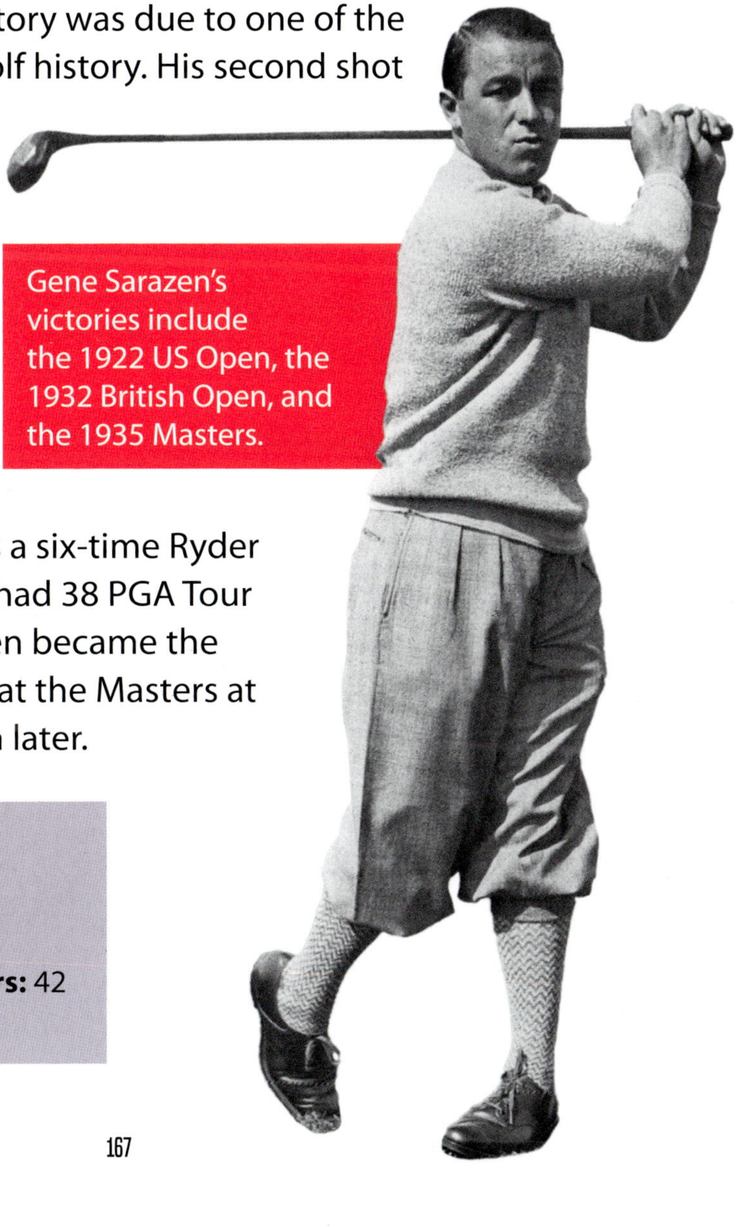

Gene Sarazen's victories include the 1922 US Open, the 1932 British Open, and the 1935 Masters.

Sarazen also invented the sand wedge golf club. He was a six-time Ryder Cup team member and had 38 PGA Tour victories. In 1999, Sarazen became the oldest Honorary Starter at the Masters at age 97. He died a month later.

Career Earnings: $76,815
Major Wins: 7
Tour Wins: 38
Top Ten Finishes in Majors: 42
Ryder Cup Record: 7–2–3

SCOTTIE SCHEFFLER

Scottie Scheffler started competing in high school, winning several state titles. In 2013, he won the US Junior Amateur Championship. Scheffler joined the developmental Korn Ferry Tour in 2019. He quickly worked his way up to the top, earning a PGA Tour spot for the 2020 season.

Scheffler's breakout year came in 2022. That year, he won several PGA Tour titles in just a few months. One was the 2022 Masters, which marked Scheffler's first time winning a major. In March 2022, Scheffler reached the top of the world golf rankings for the first time. He won back-to-back Players Championships in 2023 and 2024, and he secured a second Masters victory in 2024. That year, he competed in his first Olympic Games in Paris, France. He won gold in the men's individual stroke play event. He set an Olympic record of 19-under 265 for 72 holes. In August 2024, Scheffler held the number one spot in the world golf rankings.

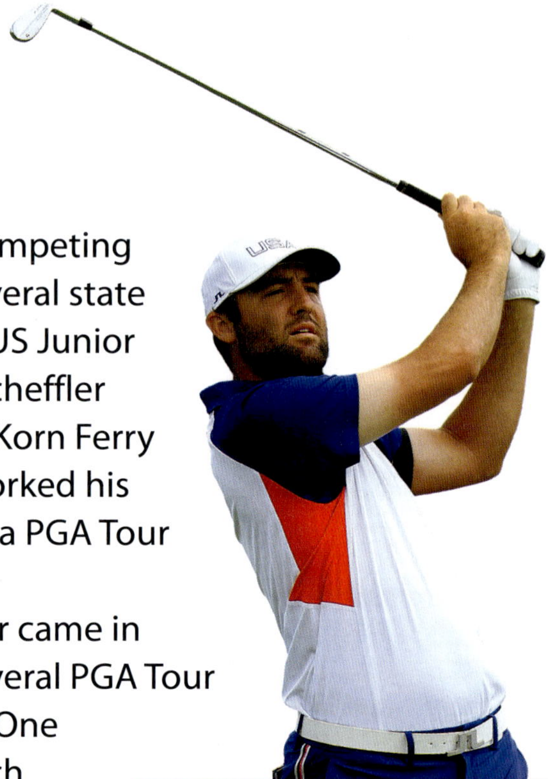

Scottie Scheffler takes a shot during the final round of the men's individual stroke play event at the 2024 Olympic Games. The tournament took place at Le Golf National in Paris, France.

Career Earnings: $71,279,258

Major Wins: 2

Tour Wins: 12

Top Ten Finishes in Majors: 12

Ryder Cup Record: 2–2–3

PATTY SHEEHAN

Patty Sheehan wasted no time making a name for herself as a professional golfer. In 1981, the Vermont native was named Rookie of the Year. During her career, she won 35 times, including six majors. The final victory of Sheehan's career was a major. It came when she won the 1996 Chevron Championship.

Sheehan was on the US Solheim Cup team four times and served as team captain twice. She is a member of three different halls of fame. For her prowess as a college golfer, she is in the Collegiate Golf Hall of Fame. She is also in the LPGA and World Golf halls of fame.

Patty Sheehan celebrates her 1996 Chevron Championship victory by jumping into Poppie's Pond at Mission Hills Country Club.

Career Earnings: $5,510,046
Major Wins: 6
Tour Wins: 35
Top Ten Finishes in Majors: N/A
Solheim Cup Record: 5–7–1

VIJAY SINGH

Career Earnings: $78,146,309
Major Wins: 3
Tour Wins: 34
Top Ten Finishes in Majors: 23
Ryder Cup Record: N/A

Vijay Singh was one of the most victorious international golfers in PGA Tour history. The Fiji native won 34 PGA events between 1993 and 2008. He won nine tournaments in 2004 on the way to his second straight season of finishing on top of the money list. That year, Singh was named Player of the Year by the PGA Tour and PGA of America. He became the number-one golfer in the world, holding the position for 32 weeks.

Singh won the PGA Championship twice and the Masters once. In 2006, Singh was inducted into the World Golf Hall of Fame. In 2013, he began playing on the PGA Tour Champions.

In 2024, Vijay Singh competed in the Galleri Classic, a PGA Tour Champions event.

Sam Snead taught himself how to play golf at a young age. He was nicknamed Slammin' Sam because he could hit the ball so far.

SAM SNEAD

Career Earnings: $713,155
Major Wins: 7
Tour Wins: 82
Top Ten Finishes in Majors: 48
Ryder Cup Record: 10–2–1

Sam Snead was known for his straw hat, humor, and self-taught swing. From 1936 to 1965, the Virginian won 82 PGA Tour events. Seven were majors, including three Masters and three PGA Championships. The only major Snead didn't win was the US Open. He finished in second place four times.

Snead won the Greater Greensboro Open eight times, the most any golfer has won a single tournament. Greensboro was also the site of Snead's final PGA Tour win in 1965. At age 52, he was the oldest golfer to ever win a PGA event. Snead found success on the PGA Tour Champions too, winning tournaments into the 1970s.

ANNIKA SÖRENSTAM

Annika Sörenstam is one of the most successful women's golfers. The Swede's first LPGA win was the 1995 US Women's Open. The next year, she won it again with a record four-round score of 272. Sörenstam won ten major championships, becoming the first to win the Women's PGA Championship three consecutive times. She completed the career grand slam before the Evian Championship became a major.

Annika Sörenstam's appearance in the 2003 Bank of America Colonial marked the first time in more than 50 years that a woman had appeared in a PGA Tour event.

Between 1995 and 2008, Sörenstam won 72 LPGA Tour events. In 2001, Sörenstam set or tied 30 records, becoming the first LPGA player to record a single-round 59. In 2003, she became the first woman to appear in a PGA Tour event since Babe Didrikson Zaharias when she played in the Bank of America Colonial.

Career Earnings: $22,583,693

Major Wins: 10

Tour Wins: 72

Top Ten Finishes in Majors: 31

Solheim Cup Record: 22–11–4

Sörenstam was also an eight-time European Solheim Cup team member and a nonplaying captain in 2017.

Sörenstam retired after the 2008 season. She held the record for most Player of the Year honors at eight. She was also the leader in career earnings with $22.5 million. That record stood 15 years after her retirement.

Annika Sörenstam competes in the 2007 Evian Championship. She finished in sixth place.

PAYNE STEWART

Payne Stewart, dressed in knickers and a tam-o'-shanter cap, celebrates after winning the 1999 US Open at Pinehurst No. 2.

During his golf career, Payne Stewart was easily recognizable for his unique outfits. He wore pants that resembled knickers and a tam-o'-shanter hat for every tournament. He also stood out for his outgoing personality, sportsmanship, and pure golf swing.

Stewart took home 11 PGA Tour titles, including three majors, and was a five-time US Ryder Cup team member. His victory in the 1999 US Open was particularly memorable. He sank a 15-foot par putt to win by one stroke over Phil Mickelson. However, Stewart died later that same year in a plane crash. He was 42 years old. Payne was inducted into the World Golf Hall of Fame in 2001.

Career Earnings: $11,737,008
Major Wins: 3
Tour Wins: 11
Top Ten Finishes in Majors: 18
Ryder Cup Record: 8–9–2

LOUISE SUGGS

Louise Suggs was a top golfer in the 1940s and 1950s. After earning several titles as an amateur, including three majors, she turned pro in 1948. By the end of 1949, Suggs won two more majors. She won 11 total majors, becoming the first woman to complete the career grand slam. She finished with 61 professional wins.

Suggs's 1949 US Women's Open win by 14 strokes is a record. She was also one of the LPGA's founders. She served as its president from 1955 to 1957. Suggs was one of the first inductees into the LPGA Hall of Fame in 1967 and was enshrined in the World Golf Hall of Fame in 1979.

Career Earnings: $190,475
Major Wins: 11
Tour Wins: 61
Top Ten Finishes in Majors: N/A
Solheim Cup Record: N/A

Louise Suggs was the leading LPGA money winner in 1953 and 1960. The LPGA's Rookie of the Year award is named after Suggs.

LEE TREVINO

At the 1968 US Open, Lee Trevino became the first golfer to shoot all four rounds of the tournament under par.

Texan Lee Trevino joined the PGA Tour in 1967, coming in fifth place at the US Open. He later won the 1968 and 1971 US Opens. It was one of three majors that Trevino won twice. He also won the 1974 and 1984 PGA Championships, and the 1971 and 1972 British Opens.

During Trevino's 1971 season, he was named PGA Player of the Year. He became the first to win the US Open, Canadian Open, and British Open in the same year. He was a six-time US Ryder Cup team member, serving as captain in 1985.

In 1975, Trevino was struck by lightning and suffered a spinal injury. But he recovered and continued to play. Trevino won 29 PGA Tour events and ranked third in career money. After joining the Champions Tour at age 50, Trevino became the first player to surpass $1 million in a single season. He won 29 times on the Champions Tour.

Career Earnings: $9,869,613

Major Wins: 6

Tour Wins: 29

Top Ten Finishes in Majors: 22

Ryder Cup Record: 17–7–6

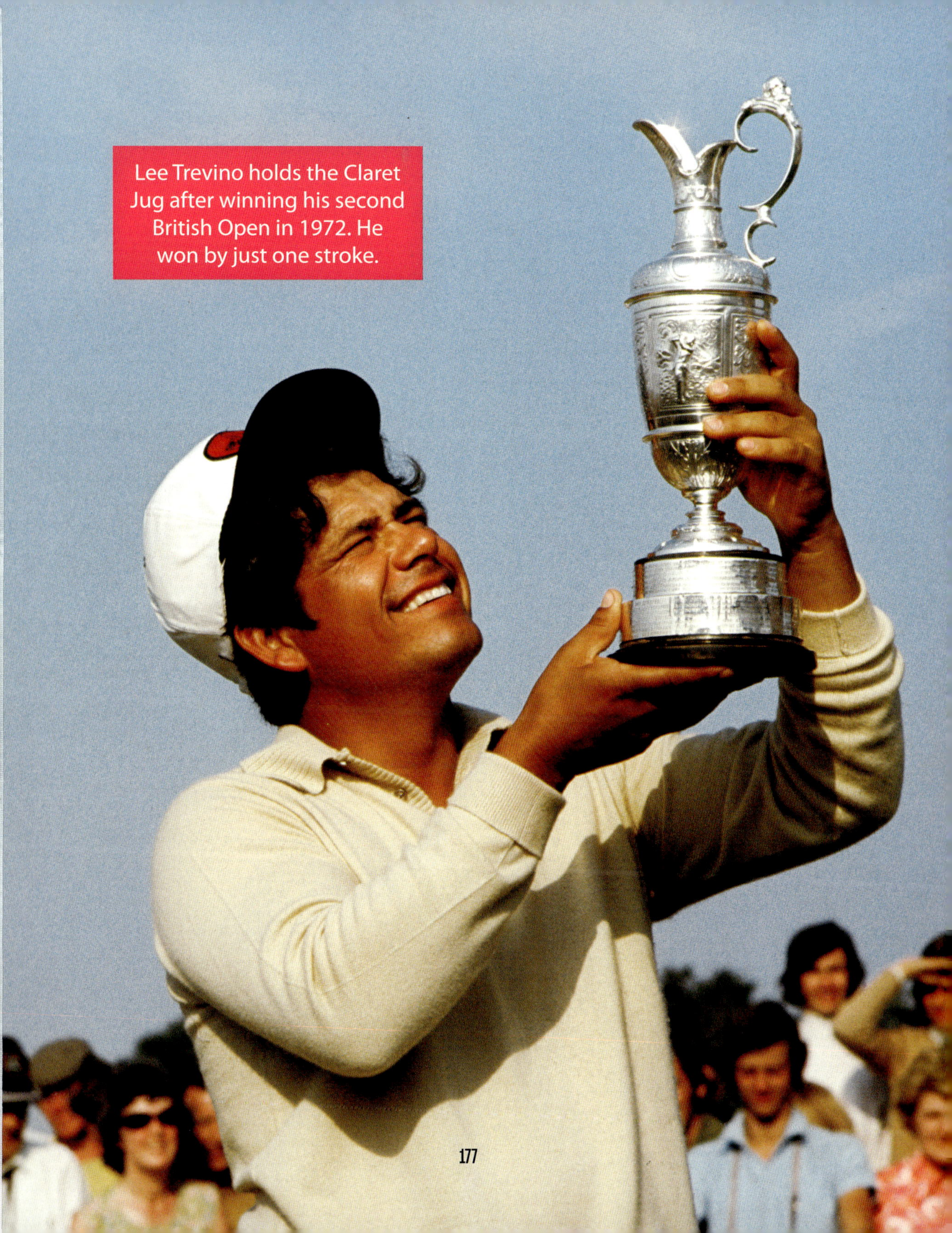

Lee Trevino holds the Claret Jug after winning his second British Open in 1972. He won by just one stroke.

HARRY VARDON

British golfer Harry Vardon was a frequent winner in the late 1800s and early 1900s. Two trophies are named after him. The Vardon Trophy goes to the PGA Tour golfer with the lowest scoring average. The Harry Vardon Trophy goes to the winner of the European Tour's Race to Dubai.

Harry Vardon was considered one of the top golfers of his day. He and fellow golfers James Braid and J. H. Taylor were known as the Great Triumvirate.

Harry Vardon, *center*, hits a shot during a 1912 tournament at Sunningdale Golf Club in Berkshire, England.

Vardon learned golf while working for an amateur golfer. When he realized he was skilled and could make money, Vardon turned pro. He went on to win the British Open six times between 1896 and 1914. He also won the 1900 US Open. Vardon's six British Open victories remain a record as of 2023.

The way Vardon hit the ball was new at the time. Instead of hitting low driving shots that had good distance but little control, Vardon hit high shots that landed and stopped quickly. This gave him more control on shorter shots, allowing him to get balls closer to the flagstick. The overlapping grip he used on his club became known as "the Vardon."

Career Earnings: N/A
Major Wins: 7
Tour Wins: 49
Top Ten Finishes in Majors: 23
Ryder Cup Record: N/A

Tom Watson, *right*, holds the Claret Jug alongside his wife, Linda, after winning his first British Open in 1975.

TOM WATSON

Tom Watson made risky but rewarding moves. His tenacity helped him win 39 times on the PGA Tour, with eight majors. He won an additional 14 times in international tournaments and the PGA Tour Champions.

Five of Watson's major wins were British Opens. This was the second-most British Open wins of all time and the most by any American. One of his British Open victories was the "Duel in the Sun," in which he defeated Jack Nicklaus. Watson defeated him again at the 1982 US Open.

Watson was the PGA Tour's leading money winner five times in his career. He was PGA Tour Player of the Year six times. On the PGA Tour Champions, Watson won six more majors. In 2015, he became the oldest player to shoot a Masters round under par at age 65.

Tom Watson competes in the 1982 US Open at Pebble Beach. He defeated Jack Nicklaus by two strokes.

Career Earnings: $30,136,954

Major Wins: 8

Tour Wins: 39

Top Ten Finishes in Majors: 46

Ryder Cup Record: 10–4–1

KARRIE WEBB

Australian Karrie Webb dominated women's golf in the late 1990s and early 2000s. She won the 1995 Women's Open on the Women's Professional Golfers' European Tour. She joined the LPGA in 1996, becoming the first rookie in men's or women's golf to surpass $1 million in a season.

Webb won the Women's Open twice before the LPGA considered it a major. She won again in 2001, giving her a career grand slam. After the Evian Championship became the LPGA's fifth major in 2013, Webb won it, becoming the only Super Career Grand Slam winner. She won 41 times on the LPGA Tour, including seven majors. She is in the LPGA and World Golf halls of fame.

Career Earnings: $20,293,617

Major Wins: 7

Tour Wins: 41

Top Ten Finishes in Majors: 36

Solheim Cup Record: N/A

Karrie Webb competes in the 2001 US Women's Open at Pine Needles Lodge and Golf Club in North Carolina. She won the tournament by eight strokes, claiming her second US Women's Open title.

Kathy Whitworth celebrates a shot during the 1985 Legends of Golf Tournament. She and Mickey Wright were the first women to play in the event.

KATHY WHITWORTH

Kathy Whitworth is the most victorious American tour golfer of all time. She and Mickey Wright were a dominating women's golf duo in the 1960s. They held a combined number of 121 victories, with 53 wins belonging to Whitworth. From 1965 to 1968, Whitworth won 35 times.

Whitworth went on to win 88 tournaments, the most by any men's or women's golfer on a US tour. In 1981, she became the first LPGA player to reach $1 million in career earnings after finishing third in the US Women's Open. It was the only major in her era that she didn't win. Whitworth died in 2022. She is in the LPGA and World Golf halls of fame.

Career Earnings: $871,296
Major Wins: 6
Tour Wins: 88
Top Ten Finishes in Majors: 33
Solheim Cup Record: 1–1–0 (nonplaying captain)

Tiger Woods celebrates after winning the 1997 Masters at Augusta National Golf Club. He won with a record score of 270, 18 under par.

TIGER WOODS

Career Earnings: $120,954,766
Major Wins: 15
Tour Wins: 82
Top Ten Finishes in Majors: 41
Ryder Cup Record: 13–21–3

Tiger Woods's three straight US Amateur titles grabbed the world's attention. So did his All-America status at Stanford University. When Woods turned pro in 1996, he was named PGA Tour Rookie of the Year and *Sports Illustrated* Sportsman of the Year.

Woods won his first major at the 1997 Masters. At age 21, he was the tournament's youngest winner and set records for lowest tournament score and largest margin of victory. Woods was also the first Black man to win the event.

Woods won 82 times on the PGA Tour. He holds the second-most major wins at 15. In 2000, Woods won the US Open, British Open, and PGA Championship. He won the 2001 Masters, becoming the only player to have all four pro majors at once. He made the cut in 142 consecutive events, breaking the record by 29 events.

Woods changed how golf was played and what professional golfers looked like. His power and distance inspired people to redesign courses. Many people emulated his dedication to fitness.

Woods competes during the 2002 US Open at Bethpage Black. He defeated Phil Mickelson to claim his second US Open title.

MICKEY WRIGHT

Career Earnings: N/A
Major Wins: 13
Tour Wins: 82
Top Ten Finishes in Majors: N/A
Solheim Cup Record: N/A

During the 1960s, Mickey Wright dominated women's golf. She and Kathy Whitworth won a combined 121 tournaments, with 68 belonging to Wright. In her 1963 season, Wright had 13 wins, the most held by a woman in a single season. She finished her career with 82 wins.

Wright is one of two four-time US Women's Open winners. She is also the only four-time LPGA Championship winner. Wright won 13 majors and was one of six women to complete the career grand slam in the four-major era. Today, the US Women's Open winner receives the Mickey Wright Medal.

Mickey Wright competes during the 1961 US Women's Open, which she later won. Wright also won the tournament in 1958, 1959, and 1964.

Mickey Wright holds several LPGA records, including the record for most wins in a single season at 13. She was also the fastest player to reach 30 victories.

Ben Hogan and Byron Nelson called Wright's swing the "greatest ever." Wright is in the LPGA and World Golf halls of fame. She died in 2020 at age 85.

GLOSSARY

advocate
Someone who works for the well-being and best interests of another person or group.

amateur
A person who does something for enjoyment without getting paid.

biennial
Taking place every other year.

bunker
A grassy or sandy area on a golf course that is used as a hazard or trap.

caddie
A person who carries a golfer's equipment during a round.

commemorate
To remember or honor.

commentator
A person who provides commentary on events such as sports.

consecutive
Following one after the other, or back-to-back.

fairway
An area of cut grass on a golf course that sits between the teeing ground and the green.

gamesmanship
The practice of winning a game or gaining an advantage in a game by using questionable methods and bending, but not breaking, the rules.

purse
The total amount of prize money offered in a sports tournament.

raucous
Loud, excited, and noisy.

rough
An area of tall grass on a golf course that borders the fairway.

stroke play
In golf, a scoring system in which the winner is determined by the total number of strokes.

sudden death
In golf, a type of tiebreaker in which the first golfer to win a hole wins the match.

tenacity
Courage and persistence.

war bond
An amount of money paid to the government to fund a war; after the war, the government would repay the money with interest.

TO LEARN MORE

FURTHER READINGS

Abdo, Kenny. *History of Golf*. Abdo, 2020.

Illustrated Sports Encyclopedia. DK, 2023.

McDougall, Chrös. *The Olympics Encyclopedia*. Abdo, 2022.

ONLINE RESOURCES

Booklinks
NONFICTION NETWORK
FREE! ONLINE NONFICTION RESOURCES

To learn more about professional golf, please visit **abdobooklinks.com** or scan this QR code. These links are routinely monitored and updated to provide the most current information available.

INDEX

PHOTO CREDITS

Cover Photos: J. D. Cuban/Allsport/Hulton Archive/Getty Images, front (Annika Sörenstam); Augusta National/Masters Historic Imagery/Getty Images, front (Arnold Palmer); Evening Standard/Hulton Archive/Getty Images, front (Ben Hogan); Phil Sandlin/AP Images, front (Jack Nicklaus); Orlando Ramirez/Getty Images Sport/Getty Images, front (Nelly Korda); Brennan Asplen/Getty Images Sport/Getty Images, front (Scottie Scheffler); Andrew Redington/Getty Images Sport/Getty Images, front (Tiger Woods); Chatchai Somwat/Shutterstock Images, back (Michelle Wie); David W. Leindecker/Shutterstock Images, back (Phil Mickelson)
Interior Photos: Mike Groll/AP Images, 1; Jan Kruger/R&A/Getty Images, 3; Chronicle/Alamy, 4; Painting/Alamy, 5; Everett Collection/Shutterstock Images, 6; Bettmann/Getty Images, 7, 12, 37, 48, 52, 120, 122, 128, 167, 176, 183; Augusta National/Masters Historic Imagery/Getty Images, 8, 25, 84, 124, 134, 146, 153; PGA Tour Archive/Getty Images, 9; Bill Waugh/AP Images, 10; Keith Hailey/Popperfoto/Getty Images, 13, 36; Harry How/Getty Images Sport/Getty Images, 14; Bob Leverone/AP Images, 15; Jennifer Perez/PGA Tour/Getty Images, 16–17; Montana Pritchard/PGA of America/Getty Images, 17; Keyur Khamar/PGA Tour/Getty Images, 18, 22, 23, 92–93 (left), 97; Andrew Medichini/AP Images, 19; Jamie Squire/Getty Images Sport/Getty Images, 20, 116; Matt Slocum/AP Images, 21; AP Images, 24, 41, 46, 50, 58, 129, 135, 139, 142, 143, 155, 156, 162, 165, 171, 180, 186; Richard Nairin/Michael Ochs Archives/Getty Images, 26; David Cannon/David Cannon Collection/Getty Images, 27, 38–39, 45, 76–77, 82, 95, 98, 100, 100–101, 145, 168; David Cannon/Allsport/David Cannon Collection/Getty Images, 28, 80, 130, 174; David J. Phillip/AP Images, 29; Stacy Revere/Getty Images Sport/Getty Images, 30, 92–93 (right); Carmen Mandato/Getty Images Sport/Getty Images, 31; John Locher/AP Images, 32; Ross Kinnaird/Getty Images Sport/Getty Images, 33, 91; Paul Popper/Popperfoto/Getty Images, 34, 56; Doug Mills/AP Images, 35; Darren Carroll/PGA of America/Getty Images, 39, 40, 87, 90; Michael Cohen/Getty Images Sport/Getty Images, 42; Andy Lyons/PGA of America/Getty Images, 43; PGA of America/Getty Images, 44–45 (left), 75, 178, 187; Andrew Redington/Getty Images Sport/Getty Images, 47, 56–57, 77, 85, 102, 104–105; Evan Vucci/AP Images, 49; Ezra Shaw/Getty Images Sport/Getty Images, 50–51, 55, 96–97; Alan Marler/AP Images, 53; Craig Jones/Allsport/Getty Images Sport/Getty Images, 54; R&A Championships/Getty Images, 59, 60; Jon Super/AP Images, 61, 66; Peter Dazeley/Getty Images Sport/Getty Images, 62; Warren Little/Getty Images Sport/Getty Images, 63, 64, 65; Oisin Keniry/R&A/Getty Images, 66–67; Andrew Redington/Allsport/Getty Images Sport/Getty Images, 68; Fabrice Coffrini/AFP/Getty Images, 69; Stuart Franklin/Getty Images Sport/Getty Images, 70–71, 71, 72–73, 73, 83, 105; Ray Illingworth/AP Images, 74; David Jensen/Icon Sportswire/AP Images, 78; Chris Carlson/AP Images, 79; Ross Parker/SNS Group/Getty Images, 80–81, 106; Patrick Smith/Getty Images Sport/Getty Images, 86; Darren Carroll/Getty Images Sport/Getty Images, 88; Richard Heathcote/Getty Images Sport/Getty Images, 89; Rob Carr/Getty Images Sport/Getty Images, 94; Tom Able-Green/Allsport/Getty Images Sport/Getty Images, 99; Peter Morrison/AP Images, 103; Matt Dunham/AP Images, 107, 136; Tony Ding/Icon Sportswire/Getty Images, 108; Charlie Riedel/AP Images, 109; Brian Spurlock/Icon Sportswire/Getty Images, 110–111; Ryan Young/PGA Tour/Getty Images, 111; Christian Petersen/Getty Images Sport/Getty Images, 112; Ben Jared/PGA Tour/Getty Images, 113; Michael Steele/EMPICS/PA Images/Getty Images, 114; Cristina Quicler/AFP/Getty Images, 114–115; Leonard Kamsler/Popperfoto/Getty Images, 117, 148, 152; Focus On Sport/Getty Images Sport/Getty Images, 118, 121, 137, 140; Steve Powell/Getty Images Sport/Getty Images, 119; Rolls Press/Popperfoto/Getty Images, 123; Frank Christian/PGA of America/Getty Images, 125; Phil Sheldon/Popperfoto/Getty Images, 126; Matt Rourke/AP Images, 127; Charlie Neibergall/AP Images, 131; S&G/PA Images Archive/Getty Images, 132; Chris Condon/PGA Tour/Getty Images, 133; Ed Widdis/AP Images, 138; Tony Roberts/Corbis Historical/Getty Images, 141; Kevin C. Cox/Getty Images Sport/Getty Images, 144; Patrick McDermott/Getty Images Sport/Getty Images, 147; Fred Kfoury III/Icon Sportswire/AP Images, 149; Dave Martin/AP Images, 150, 172; David W. Leindecker/Shutterstock Images, 151; Tom Sande/AP Images, 154; Phil Sandlin/AP Images, 157; Stan Badz/PGA Tour/Getty Images, 158; Stephen Dunn/Getty Images Sport/Getty Images, 159; Andy Lyons/Allsport/Getty Images Sport/Getty Images, 160; Harry How/Allsport/Getty Images Sport/Getty Images, 161; Bob Thomas/Bob Thomas Sports Photography/Getty Images, 163; Shutterstock Images, 164, 173; Pictorial Parade/Archive Photos/Getty Images, 166; Stephen Dunn/Allsport/Hulton Archive/Getty Images, 169; Orlando Ramirez/Getty Images Sport/Getty Images, 170; Julian Graham/PGA of America/Getty Images, 175; PA Images/Getty Images, 177; Topical Press Agency/Hulton Archive/Getty Images, 178–179; John Kelly/Getty Images Sport/Getty Images, 181; Erik Perel/AFP/Getty Images, 182; Curtis Compton/AP Images, 184; Mark Lennihan/AP Images, 185

ABDOBOOKS.COM
Published by Abdo Reference, a division of ABDO, PO Box 398166, Minneapolis, Minnesota 55439.

Printed in China.
102024
012025

THIS BOOK CONTAINS RECYCLED MATERIALS

Editor: Laura Stickney
Series Designer: Colleen McLaren
Production Designer: Joshua Olson

LIBRARY OF CONGRESS CONTROL NUMBER: 2024938493

PUBLISHER'S CATALOGING-IN-PUBLICATION DATA
Names: Stathes, Corbu, author.
Title: The professional golf encyclopedia / by Corbu Stathes
Description: Minneapolis, Minnesota: Abdo Reference, 2025 | Series: Sports encyclopedias | Includes online resources and index.
Identifiers: ISBN 9781098296100 (lib. bdg.) | ISBN 9798384917106 (eBook)
Subjects: LCSH: Professional Golfers' Association of America--Juvenile literature. | Professional sports--Juvenile literature. | Athletics--Juvenile literature. | Golf--Juvenile literature. | Sports--History--Juvenile literature.
Classification: DDC 796.352--dc23